History Department
King City Secondary School

The Advent of Civilization

PROBLEMS IN EUROPEAN CIVILIZATION

Under the editorial direction of
John Ratté
Amherst College

The Advent of Civilization

Edited and with an introduction by

Wayne M. Bledsoe
University of Missouri—Rolla

D. C. HEATH AND COMPANY
Lexington, Massachusetts   Toronto   London

CONTENTS

IV CIVILIZATION: A RADIANT LIGHT?

INTRODUCTION

Marc Bloch, the noted authority on medieval feudalism, once observed that "behind the visible characteristics of the countryside, the tools and the machines, behind writings—even those which appear to be the most completely detached from the people who established them—it is men that history seeks to grasp." Bloch's truism, like most, is more easily theorized than realized. While the natural object of history may be man, the historian soon discovers that his quarry is both elusive and protean. The historian who attempts to realize Bloch's historical objective by tracing man's odyssey through successive periods of time may soon discover that his chameleon prey has vanished within the maze of visible characteristics that surrounds him. Perhaps a more fruitful approach is to be found in Lord Acton's dictum that historians should concentrate on problems rather than periods. When man is viewed in light of a historical problem of the highest magnitude, an understanding of his nature, capabilities, and limitations becomes a distinct possibility. The question of how man was able to bridge the yawning gap between primitive society and civilization is just such a problem.

As is the case with almost all historical problems of major consequence, there has never been and there is not now agreement on the nature and the significance of the rise of civilization. The selections that follow will show not only a difference of opinion concerning what happened nearly five thousand years ago, but will also provide a clear indication of what has been the source of disagreement dividing the historians, archaeologists, anthropologists, sociologists and theologians who have tried to explain how man made the transformation to what we call civilization. The questions posed by the sources are simple, yet fundamental. How did civilization come about? What animus impelled man to forego the independence, intimacies, and invariability of tribal existence for the much larger and more impersonal political complexity we call the state? What forces fused to initiate the mutation that slowly transformed nomadic campsites into populous cities with ethnic mixtures, stratified societies, diversified economies, organized religious cults and unique cultural forms? Was the advent of civilization the inevitable result of social evolution and natural laws of progress or was man the designer of his own destiny? Have technological innovations been the motivating force or was it some intangible factor such as religion or intellectual advancement?

Until the mid-nineteenth century, Western man was only little troubled by the issue of civilization. Most people in the previous two centuries had rested comfortably in the theory advanced by Archbishop John Ussher and Dr. John Lightfoot, that civilization started in 4004 B.C. with the creation of man. Between the historical act of creation and his own day, the reflective individual had a vague sense of the four world empires of Assyria, Persia, Greece and Rome, which was followed by a prolonged period of Christian dominance in the West. Within this early concept of civilization, whenever it became necessary for man to account for a gap of time that was prehistory, this was frequently achieved by simply inventing ancestors or by conjuring up a mythical past filled with descendants of the heroic Greeks and Trojans. For those antiquaries preferring a more direct Biblical heritage there were always the sons of Japhet, who were reported to be the first farmers in Europe, or the Ten Lost Tribes of Israel. However the story was told, by the early nineteenth century man was not only confident of where he stood but was reasonably certain how he got there. He believed that modern man stood at the pinnacle of a long and glorious heritage he loosely labeled Western civilization. Athens had provided the intellectual and artistic heritage, Rome provided the judicial and civil guidance, and Jerusalem supplied the faith and morals. This over-simplified story of civilization was not seriously shaken until the nineteenth century, when virtually forgotten civilizations began to yield their secrets to the spade of the archaeologist and much that had been long dismissed as myth was substantiated.

As the archaeologists were busily digging up material evidence of man's remote past, the anthropologists and ethnographers were refining existing theories on the development of primitive societies. Through the utilization of theoretical models and Darwin's views on biological evolution, anthropologists sought to demonstrate that there were three general stages in man's social and cultural evolution—savagery, barbarism, and finally civilization. The framework for analyzing the prehistoric culture sequence was, by the late nineteenth century, formalized in terms of a belief in cultural evolution and laws of human progress. The newly discovered prehistoric records the archaeologists were studying seemed to harmonize adequately with the doctrines set forth by anthropologists.

Although there were some minor discrepancies between the theoretical models of the anthropologists and models based on material evidence of the archaeologists, the labor of the two seems to have dovetailed in the work of the American anthropologist, Lewis Henry Morgan. Morgan, a unilateral evolutionist, worked out a detailed formula to illustrate the progressive sequence of man's cultural evolution. In his *Ancient Society: Research in the Lines of Human Progress from Savagery through Barbarism to Civilization* (1877) he distinguished seven ethnic periods in the human past: Lower Savagery, from the emergence of man to the discovery of fire; Middle Savagery, from the discovery of fire to the discovery of the bow and arrow; Upper Savagery, from the bow and arrow to pottery; Lower Barbarism, from the discovery of pottery to the domestication of animals; Middle Barbarism, from the domestication of animals to the smelting of iron ore; Upper Barbarism, from the discovery of iron to the invention of the phonetic alphabet; his seventh and last stage, from writing and the alphabet onwards, was civilization.

Needless to say, the nineteenth century did not experience universal agreement on the views set forth by the evolutionists. Christianity in particular felt threatened because the theory of cultural evolution and the three stages of man's development contradicted the Genesis account of creation. While there were various responses to the evolutionists, one of the more sophisticated was that of Archbishop Richard Whately. He maintained, in his essay on "Origins of Civilization" (1881), that while it was possible to document periods of savagery and barbarism in man's past, these had not been his original state. Man had been created at a relatively high level of civilization, which was followed by a period of degeneration. It was from this degenerate state that man was forced to begin his progress back toward civilization. Whately's analysis represents an effort to retain the Genesis account of creation without denying the theory of progress.

The flames of enthusiasm kindled by the new discoveries of the archaeologists soon took on new dimensions that were reflected in a rich debate over the issues of cultural diffusion and the question of where civilization originated. This debate was precipitated by the discovery of similar cultural traits in different parts of the world. Did this similarity in cultural patterns mean that man's transformation occurred only once, and that from a common nucleus the roots of civilization were transported around the world, or did the rise of civilization actually have multiple beginnings with identical characteristics? With an ardor bordering on religious zeal, the Egyptocentric G. Elliot Smith responded to this question on the advent of civilization with his still famous hyperdiffusionist theory. Elliot Smith argued with conviction that the rise of civilization occurred once and only once and that the phenomenon took place in Egypt. Civilization was born on the banks of the Nile and diffused from there to Mesopotamia, the Indus Valley, to China, and even further, across the Pacific to Central America. The key to his unilineal doctrine was mummification. It was Smith's opinion that the scientific and technological aspects of embalming were too complex to have had multiple beginnings. As a result, any practice of embalming or mummification, whether in the Old World or New, was thought to have spread from Egypt.

The Elliot Smith school found a kindred spirit, though not a disciple, in Lord Raglan. Two years after the death of Smith (1937) Raglan published his *How Came Civilization?* in which he supported the hyperdiffusionist thesis, but shifted the center of civilization from Egypt to the banks of the Tigris-Euphrates. He maintained that the Sumerians, not the Egyptians, were the heralds of civilization. His pan-Sumerian thesis rested upon the belief that no invention, discovery, custom or belief is known to have originated in two separate cultures. The natural state of man, according to Raglan, was a low state of savagery, and the savage never invented anything. He viewed the principal discoveries and inventions of civilization as having their origins in Mesopotamia and then diffused from there.

Although the hyperdiffusionists are still with us, the pan-Egyptian and pan-Sumerian theses have been seriously weakened. Rushton

Coulborn, in *The Origin of Civilized Societies* (1959), summarily dismissed the contention of the hyperdiffusionists that the advent of civilization was a unique phenomenon that occurred only once, and discounted their assumption that things cannot be discovered or invented more than once. Following the lead of Arnold Toynbee and Alfred Weber, Coulborn saw not one, but seven primary civilizations. He maintained that diffusion had nothing to do with the origin of the seven primary civilized societies as there is clear evidence that each originated independently and each produced its own distinct "style."

A more personal response to Elliot Smith and Lord Raglan is Glyn Daniel's "Diffusion and Distraction" (1962). With regard to the hyperdiffusionist doctrine in general, Daniel established two fundamental reasons why what he calls "academic rubbish" is tolerated. First, there is man's ever-present and deep-seated desire for simple, all-embracing solutions to complex problems. While there is nothing inherently wrong with simple solutions, those of the hyperdiffusionists were simplistic and, consequently, unacceptable. A second reason for the public tolerance of simplistic historical answers, such as those of Smith and Raglan, can be attributed to the intense bewilderment felt by a society confronted with increased quantities of archaeological evidence which cannot be juxtaposed satisfactorily. As man's bewilderment has increased, so have his efforts to find a magical key to the remote past at such places as the lost islands of Atlantis or Mu, or, as a more recent thesis has attempted, by linking the rise of civilization to the possibility of prehistoric interplanetary space travel. Along with his criticism of Smith and Raglan, Daniel interjects an important note of caution. Diffusion, he maintained, as an explanation of cultural change is not an error; the error is obsessional extremes of using diffusion, *or* evolution, as the only explanation for cultural change.

The new prehistory of the past half-century has labored to rectify the excesses of the hyperdiffusionists and evolutionists, with one of the consequences being an elevated role for man in determining his own destiny. Although the advances made in contemporary prehistoric studies reflect the labors of a host of specialists working in a variety of disciplines, the image of the eminent archaeologist V. Gordon Childe looms large. In his very provocative *Man Makes Himself* (1936), Childe insists upon the necessity of differentiating between historical progress and organic evolution. In essence, Childe advocated a modified diffusion theory in which man filled the dual role of both architect and transmitter of civilization. He maintained that "change in culture and tradition can be initiated, controlled, or delayed by the conscious and deliberate choice of their human author and executor." Invention, he said, was not an accidental mutation of germ plasm, ". . . but a new synthesis of the accumulated experience to which the inventor was heir by tradition only." The coming of civilization, which he equates to the rise of the city, or, in his terms, "the Urban Revolution," was precipitated by a series of epoch-making inventions that prepared man for urban life and provided sufficient subsistence for that complexity we call civilization. A self-proclaimed Marxist, Childe spiced his work with materialistic emphasis, such as the nineteen basic discoveries that he linked with the "Urban Revolution," which in the final analysis reflect his basic contention that the coming of civilization is the story of man "finding himself, expressing himself, making himself."

In the context of contemporary prehistoric studies, Childe's *Man Makes Himself* may be viewed as a veritable stormy petrel. While few scholars fully agree with his conclusions, even fewer have been able to ignore him. The extent and nature of the diverse controversy engendered by Childe is reflected in the works of Grahame Clark and Robert Redfield. Clark, in his *Aspects of Prehistory* (1970), concluded that it was not only incorrect to maintain that man made himself, but also that the conclusion was unscientific. Clark, an anthropologist, is particularly perturbed by the fact that a fellow scientist would lend credence to the inane humanist view of man as the creator of his own destiny by providing an anthropomorphic explanation of prehistory. Man, the universe, and all other forms of life, he believed, were part of an all-embracing evolutionary process, and to extract man from the process was senseless. He is quite adamant in his belief that man and his way of life are both ultimately the product of natural selection.

While Grahame Clark considers the Childe thesis to be an anathema for its unscientific conclusions, the noted sociologist Robert Redfield takes issue with Childe for other reasons. According to Redfield, when Childe refers to "man making himself" the reference is to an ongoing technological phenomenon that appears to have been unplanned. It is Childe looking backward at the prehistoric technological advancements who sees man as a versatile inventor, and the ultimate consequence—civilization—was actually the natural result of material progress.

Redfield's opinion is that if man is truly the maker of himself it must be demonstrated that the coming of civilization was not just a happy coincidence, but rather the result of deliberate intention and design. The basic question posed by Redfield is simple. In the transformation of folk society into civilization, does man control the process and direct it where he wills? Through an investigation of the origin and development of the idea of reform, Redfield concludes that primitive man was not concerned with transforming his society but rather he "looks toward a future that reproduces the immediate past." The intentional making over of society is a conception of modern origins, and to present primitive man as the conscious shaper of his own destiny is an error. Viewed from the intellectual perspective of Redfield, primitive man cannot be seen as "making himself."

There is yet another dimension added by Robert M. Adams to our already conflicting views. In *The Evolution of Urban Society* (1966), Adams expressed concern over the distortions emitting from Childe's use of the term "Urban Revolution." The word revolution immediately conjures up images of a conscious struggle. Such an implication might be appropriate when applied to a few specific events, but it is inappropriate when applied to the advent of civilization in general. He also disagrees with Childe's contention that civilization must be equated with urbanization. "At least as a form of settlement . . . urbanism seems to have been much less important to the emergence of the state, and even to the development of civilization in the broadest sense, than social stratification and the institutionalization of political authority." In conclusion, Adams believes the change most fundamental to the Urban Revolution was a change in social institutions "that precipitated changes in technology, subsistence and other aspects of the wider cultural realm, rather than vice versa."

The absence, to this point, of any mention of religion as a major force in the rise of civilization is not to imply a lack of contemporary spokesmen. Henry Bamford Parkes, in his *Gods and Men* (1959), presents a very strong argument for the proposition that all the various characteristics previously associated with the rise of civilization— such as technological advancement, large economic reserves, division of labor, increase in classes with specialized functions—would have been impossible without first the presence of effective leader ship. This leadership, he believed, was provided by priests or priest-kings. Parkes maintains that as man took his first step toward civilization and encountered the anxieties of a more complex existence, he sought security through a close dependence upon divine powers. "Man's first answer to the social and political problems involved in the rise of civilization was to strip himself of all responsibility for his own destiny and project all authority upon the gods." The chief factors that made possible the rise of civilization were the social and institutional changes initiated and supervised by the representatives of a god or gods.

Possibly some word is needed concerning the impact which the advent of civilization had upon man. The views expressed by Lewis Mumford should be of particular interest in that they are contrary to the (at least implicit) creative, progressive notions set forth in the above selections. In *The Transformations of Man* (1957), Mumford emphasizes the fact that civilization was not a gift, but came at a very high price. In many respects civilization can be viewed as one long affront to human dignity. With the rise of civilization man lost the independence, intimacies and security of tribal existence. He found himself sinking into an ever-increasing sea of humanity whom he could never know intimately. Mumford maintains that with his relative anonymity civilized man became a selfish hoarder and engaged "in bestitudes and butcheries that primitive societies lacked the animus as well as the power to inflict." Along with all the advantages, hopes and promises of civilization, the transformation had its ugly side.

Contained within the aforementioned material is a century of debate whereby scholars from a variety of disciplines have attempted to assess the origins of civilization and explain man's role in the process. Although our picture is still lacking any serene unanimity of thought, the student should not be wearied by the diversity of opinion or intimidated by the thunderous rhetoric, for such is the nature of all intellectual problems dealing with the essence of life. Instead, the reader should be encouraged by the fact that any attempt to unravel the mysteries surrounding the advent of civilization is an intellectual adventure and, like all adventures, encompasses both the seeds of uncertainty and the prospects of new discovery. As each of us is made increasingly aware of the pejorative state of our own society, it should be the hope of new discovery that motivates us to address once again the question of how came civilization. Perhaps by vicariously entering the dim centuries of man's beginnings we may eventually embrace those elements, both human and physical, that are most crucial to civilization. In the process we may help alleviate the present quandary about human destiny.

Conflict of Opinion

I. Civilization: Creation, Degeneration, and Progress.

The latest investigations respecting the early conditions of the human race, are tending to the conclusion that mankind commenced their career at the bottom of the scale and worked their way up from savagery to civilization through the slow accumulation of experimental knowledge.

LEWIS HENRY MORGAN

Facts are stubborn things and that no authenticated instances can be produced of savages that ever did emerge unaided, from that state is no theory but a statement, hitherto never disproved, of a matter of fact . . . savages are degenerate descendants of civilized men.

ARCHBISHOP RICHARD WHATELY

II. Civilization: Unilineal or Multiple Beginnings?

. . . There can be no doubt the people who introduced the Neolithic culture into Europe derived most of its elements directly or indirectly from Egypt, which thus affected at their source the very springs of European civilization.

G. ELLIOT SMITH

. . . We have seen that many of the principal discoveries and inventions upon which our civilization is based can be traced with considerable probability to an area with its focus near the head of the Persian Gulf. . . .

LORD RAGLAN

Diffusion was never a cause or means of origins of a civilized society, but only a vehicle of its spread. . . . Traits and complexes diffused from other civilized societies, and from primitive societies as well, were received from time to time, but there is no evidence whatever that any of the seven societies began as a mere colony . . . sent out by another civilized society.

RUSHTON COULBORN

Now why does the world tolerate this academic rubbish from people like Elliot Smith, Perry, and Raglan? There are many reasons. First there is a deep-seated desire for a simple answer to complicated problems . . . and also because the gradual elaboration and complication of the archaeological record had begun to bewilder people.

GLYN DANIEL

III. *Civilization: Man Makes Himself.*

Between 6000 and 3000 B.C. man has learned to harness the force of oxen and of winds, he invents the plow, the wheeled cart and the sailboat, he discovers the chemical process involved in smelting copper ores and the physical properties of metals, and he begins to work out an accurate solar calendar. He has thereby equipped himself for urban life, and prepares the way for a civilization. . . .

V. GORDON CHILDE

Only a generation ago, Gordon Childe entitled a still famous book *Man Makes Himself.* . . . It is plain that if we accept the full implications of *The Origin of the Species,* if we acknowledge without reserve that man and his works are in truth a product of the same evolutionary forces as have shaped the universe, then we can hardly view him as making himself. . . .

GRAHAME CLARK

The "making of man" with which Childe is concerned is unplanned. . . . It is Childe, looking backward upon what happened in history, who sees man as the maker of himself. . . . [My] topic is the transformation of the folk society into civilization . . . by deliberate intention and design.

ROBERT REDFIELD

And it clearly was Childe's view that the primary motivating force for the transformation lay in the rise of new technological and subsistence patterns. . . . But . . . I . . . believe that the available evidence supports the conclusion that the transformation at the core of the Urban Revolution lay in the realm of social organization. . . .

ROBERT McC. ADAMS

Man's first answer to social and political problems involved in the rise of civilization was to strip himself of all responsibility for his own destiny and project all authority upon the gods. . . . Thus, the early civilizations were permeated with religion. . . .

HENRY BAMFORD PARKES

IV. *Civilization: A Radiant Light?*

Economically, the new order was based largely on the forcible exploitation of cultivators and artisans by an armed and ever-threatening minority. . . . This systematic subordination of life to its mechanical and legal agents existed at the beginning of civilization and still haunts every existing society. . . . In that sense, civilization is one long affront to human dignity.

LEWIS MUMFORD

I CIVILIZATION: CREATION, DEGENERATION, AND PROGRESS

Lewis Henry Morgan
THE LINES OF HUMAN PROGRESS

One of the first impressive attempts to provide a scientific account of the advent of civilization was Lewis Henry Morgan's Ancient Society *(1877). A jurist by profession, Morgan never served on the staff of any educational institution, yet he has been proclaimed the "Father of American Anthropology." His pioneer investigations into the culture of the American Indian resulted in a comprehensive theory of social evolution in which he advanced the doctrine of the common origin and psychic unity of all the races of men, and asserted that the career of mankind had passed through three successive stages: savagery, barbarism, and civilization. His view is that of a unilineal evolutionist.*

The latest investigations respecting the early condition of the human race, are tending to the conclusion that mankind commenced their career at the bottom of the scale and worked their way up from savagery to civilization through the slow accumulations of experimental knowledge.

As it is undeniable that portions of the human family have existed in a state of savagery, other portions in a state of barbarism, and still other portions in a state of civilization, it seems equally so that these three distinct conditions are connected with each other in a natural as well as necessary sequence of progress. Moreover, that this sequence has been historically true of the entire human family, up to the status attained by each branch respectively, is rendered probable by the conditions under which all progress occurs, and by the known advancement of several branches of the family through two or more of these conditions.

An attempt will be made in the following pages to bring forward additional evidence of the rudeness of the early condition of mankind, of the gradual evolution of their mental and moral powers through experience, and of their protracted struggle with opposing obstacles while winning their way to civilization. It will be drawn, in part, from the great sequence of inventions and discoveries which stretches along the entire pathway of human progress; but chiefly

Reprinted from Lewis Henry Morgan, *Ancient Society* (New York: Henry Holt and Company, 1878), pp. 3–13.

from domestic institutions, which express the growth of certain ideas and passions.

As we re-ascend along the several lines of progress toward the primitive ages of mankind, and eliminate one after the other, in the order in which they appeared, inventions and discoveries on the one hand, and institutions on the other, we are enabled to perceive that the former stand to each other in progressive, and the latter in unfolding relations. While the former class have had a connection, more or less direct, the latter have been developed from a few primary germs of thought. Modern institutions plant their roots in the period of barbarism, into which their germs were transmitted from the previous period of savagery. They have had a lineal descent through the ages, with the streams of the blood, as well as a logical development.

Two independent lines of investigation thus invite our attention. The one leads through inventions and discoveries, and the other through primary institutions. With the knowledge gained therefrom, we may hope to indicate the principal stages of human development. The proofs to be adduced will be drawn chiefly from domestic institutions; the references to achievements more strictly intellectual being general as well as subordinate.

The facts indicate the gradual formation and subsequent development of certain ideas, passions, and aspirations. Those which hold the most prominent positions may be generalized as growths of the particular ideas with which they severally stand connected. Apart from inventions and discoveries they are the following:

I. Subsistence   V. Religion
II. Government   VI. House Life and Architecture
III. Language   VII. Property
IV. The Family

First. Subsistence has been increased and perfected by a series of successive arts, introduced at long intervals of time, and connected more or less directly with inventions and discoveries.

Second. The germ of government must be sought in the organization into gentes in the Status of savagery; and followed down, through the advancing forms of this institution, to the establishment of political society.

Third. Human speech seems to have been developed from the

rudest and simplest forms of expression. Gesture or sign language, as intimated by Lucretius, must have preceded articulate language, as thought preceded speech. The monosyllabical preceded the syllabical, as the latter did that of concrete words. Human intelligence, unconscious of design, evolved articulate language by utilizing the vocal sounds. This great subject, a department of knowledge by itself, does not fall within the scope of the present investigation.

Fourth. With respect to the family, the stages of its growth are embodied in systems of consanguinity and affinity, and in usages relating to marriage, by means of which, collectively, the family can be definitely traced through several successive forms.

Fifth. The growth of religious ideas is environed with such intrinsic difficulties that it may never receive a perfectly satisfactory exposition. Religion deals so largely with the imaginative and emotional nature, and consequently with such uncertain elements of knowledge, that all primitive religions are grotesque and to some extent unintelligible. This subject also falls without the plan of this work excepting as it may prompt incidental suggestions.

Sixth. House architecture, which connects itself with the form of the family and the plan of domestic life, affords a tolerably complete illustration of progress from savagery to civilization. Its growth can be traced from the hut of the savage, through the communal houses of the barbarians, to the house of the single family of civilized nations, with all the successive links by which one extreme is connected with the other. This subject will be noticed incidentally.

Lastly. The idea of property was slowly formed in the human mind, remaining nascent and feeble through immense periods of time. Springing into life in savagery, it required all the experience of this period and of the subsequent period of barbarism to develop the germ, and to prepare the human brain for the acceptance of its controlling influence. Its dominance as a passion over all other passions marks the commencement of civilization. It not only led mankind to overcome the obstacles which delayed civilization, but to establish political society on the basis of territory and of property. A critical knowledge of the evolution of the idea of property would embody, in some respects, the most remarkable portion of the mental history of mankind.

It will be my object to present some evidence of human progress along these several lines, and through successive ethnical periods, as it is revealed by inventions and discoveries, and by the growth of the ideas of government, of the family, and of property.

It may be here premised that all forms of government are reducible to two general plans, using the word plan in its scientific sense. In their bases the two are fundamentally distinct. The first, in the order of time, is founded upon persons, and upon relations purely personal, and may be distinguished as a society (*societas*). The gens is the unit of this organization; giving as the successive stages of integration, in the archaic period, the gens, the phratry, the tribe, and the confederacy of tribes, which constituted a people or nation (*populus*). At a later period a coalescence of tribes in the same area into a nation took the place of a confederacy of tribes occupying independent areas. Such, through prolonged ages, after the gens appeared, was the substantially universal organization of ancient society; and it remained among the Greeks and Romans after civilization supervened. The second is founded upon territory and upon property, and may be distinguished as a state (*civitas*). The township or ward, circumscribed by metes and bounds, with the property it contains, is the basis or unit of the latter, and political society is the result. Political society is organized upon territorial areas, and deals with property as well as with persons through territorial relations. The successive stages of integration are the township or ward, which is the unit of organization; the county or province, which is an aggregation of townships or wards; and the national domain or territory, which is an aggregation of counties or provinces; the people of each of which are organized into a body politic. It taxed the Greeks and Romans to the extent of their capacities, after they had gained civilization, to invent the deme or township and the city ward; and thus inaugurate the second great plan of government, which remains among civilized nations to the present hour. In ancient society this territorial plan was unknown. When it came in it fixed the boundary line between ancient and modern society, as the distinction will be recognized in these pages.

It may be further observed that the domestic institutions of the barbarous, and even of the savage ancestors of mankind, are still exemplified in portions of the human family with such completeness that, with the exception of the strictly primitive period, the several stages of this progress are tolerably well preserved. They are seen in the organization of society upon the basis of sex, then upon the basis of kin, and finally upon the basis of territory; through the successive forms of marriage and of the family, with the systems of consanguinity thereby created; through house life and architecture; and through progress in usages with respect to the ownership and inheritance of property.

The theory of human degradation to explain the existence of savages and of barbarians is no longer tenable. It came in as a corollary from the Mosaic cosmogony, and was acquiesced in from a supposed necessity which no longer exists. As a theory, it is not only incapable of explaining the existence of savages, but it is without support in the facts of human experience.

The remote ancestors of the Aryan nations presumptively passed through an experience similar to that of existing barbarous and savage tribes. Though the experience of these nations embodies all the information necessary to illustrate the periods of civilization, both ancient and modern, together with a part of that in the Later period of barbarism, their anterior experience must be deduced, in the main, from the traceable connection between the elements of their existing institutions and inventions, and similar elements still preserved in those of savage and barbarous tribes.

It may be remarked finally that the experience of mankind has run in nearly uniform channels; that human necessities in similar conditions have been substantially the same; and that the operations of the mental principle have been uniform in virtue of the specific identity of the brain of all the races of mankind. This, however, is but a part of the explanation of uniformity in results. The germs of the principal institutions and arts of life were developed while man was still a savage. To a very great extent the experience of the subsequent periods of barbarism and of civilization have been expended in the further development of these original conceptions. Wherever a connection can be traced on different continents between a present institution and a common germ, the derivation of the people themselves from a common original stock is implied.

The discussion of these several classes of facts will be facilitated by the establishment of a certain number of Ethnical Periods; each representing a distinct condition of society, and distinguishable by a mode of life peculiar to itself. The terms "Age of *Stone*," "of *Bronze*," and "of *Iron*," introduced by Danish archaeologists, have been extremely useful for certain purposes, and will remain so for the classification of objects of ancient art; but the progress of knowledge has rendered other and different subdivisions necessary. Stone implements were not entirely laid aside with the introduction of tools of iron, nor of those of bronze. The invention of the process of smelting iron ore created an ethnical epoch, yet we could scarcely date another from the production of bronze. Moreover, since the period of stone implements overlaps those of bronze and of iron, and since that of bronze also overlaps that of iron, they are not capable of a circumscription that would leave each independent and distinct.

It is probable that the successive arts of subsistence which arose at long intervals will ultimately, from the great influence they must have exercised upon the condition of mankind, afford the most satisfactory bases for these divisions. But investigation has not been carried far enough in this direction to yield the necessary information. With our present knowledge the main result can be attained by selecting such other inventions or discoveries as will afford sufficient tests of progress to characterize the commencement of successive ethnical periods. Even though accepted as provisional, these periods will be found convenient and useful. Each of those about to be proposed will be found to cover a distinct culture, and to represent a particular mode of life.

The period of savagery, of the early part of which very little is known, may be divided, provisionally, into three subperiods. These may be named respectively the *Older,* the *Middle,* and the *Later* period of savagery; and the condition of society in each, respectively, may be distinguished as the *Lower,* the *Middle,* and the *Upper Status* of savagery.

In like manner, the period of barbarism divides naturally into three subperiods, which will be called, respectively, the *Older,* the *Middle,* and the *Later* period of barbarism; and the condition of society in each, respectively, will be distinguished as the *Lower,* the *Middle,* and the *Upper Status* of barbarism.

It is difficult, if not impossible, to find such tests of progress to mark the commencement of these several periods as will be found absolute in their application, and without exceptions upon all the continents. Neither is it necessary, for the purpose in hand, that exceptions should not exist. It will be sufficient if the principal tribes of mankind can be classified, according to the degree of their relative progress, into conditions which can be recognized as distinct.

I. *Lower Status of Savagery.* This period commenced with the infancy of the human race, and may be said to have ended with the acquisition of a fish subsistence and of knowledge of the use of fire. Mankind were then living in their original restricted habitat, and subsisting upon fruits and nuts. The commencement of articulate speech belongs to this period. No exemplification of tribes of mankind in this condition remained to the historical period.

II. *Middle Status of Savagery.* It commenced with the acquisition of a fish subsistence and a knowledge of the use of fire, and ended with the invention of the bow and arrow. Mankind, while in this condition, spread from their original habitat over the greater portion of the earth's surface. Among tribes still existing it will leave in the Middle Status of savagery, for example, the Australians and the greater part of the Polynesians when discovered. It will be sufficient to give one or more exemplifications of each status.

III. *Upper Status of Savagery.* It commenced with the invention of the bow and arrow, and ended with the invention of the art of pottery. It leaves in the Upper Status of savagery the Athapascan tribes of the Hudson's Bay Territory, the tribes of the valley of the Columbia, and certain coast tribes of North and South America; but with relation to the time of their discovery. This closes the period of Savagery.

IV. *Lower Status of Barbarism.* The invention or practice of the art of pottery, all things considered, is probably the most effective and conclusive test that can be selected to fix a boundary line, necessarily arbitrary, between savagery and barbarism. The distinctness of the two conditions has long been recognized, but no criterion of progress out of the former into the latter has hitherto been brought forward. All such tribes, then, as never attained to the art of pottery will be classed as savages, and those possessing this art but who never attained a phonetic alphabet and the use of writing will be classed as barbarians.

The first subperiod of barbarism commenced with the manufacture of pottery, whether by original invention or adoption. In finding its termination, and the commencement of the Middle Status, a difficulty is encountered in the unequal endowments of the two hemispheres, which began to be influential upon human affairs after the period of savagery had passed. It may be met, however, by the adoption of equivalents. In the Eastern hemisphere, the domestication of animals, and in the Western, the cultivation of maize and plants by irrigation, together with the use of adobe-brick and stone in house building have been selected as sufficient evidence of progress to work a transition out of the Lower and into the Middle Status of barbarism. It leaves, for example, in the Lower Status, the Indian tribes of the United States east of the Missouri River, and such tribes of Europe and Asia as practiced the art of pottery, but were without domestic animals.

V. *Middle Status of Barbarism.* It commenced with the domestication of animals in the Eastern hemisphere, and in the Western with cultivation by irrigation and with the use of adobe-brick and stone in architecture, as shown. Its termination may be fixed with the invention of the process of smelting iron ore. This places in the Middle Status, for example, the Village Indians of New Mexico, Mexico, Central America and Peru, and such tribes in the Eastern hemisphere as possessed domestic animals, but were without a knowledge of iron. The ancient Britons, although familiar with the use of iron, fairly belong in this connection. The vicinity of more advanced continental tribes had advanced the arts of life among them far beyond the state of development of their domestic institutions.

VI. *Upper Status of Barbarism.* It commenced with the manufacture of iron, and ended with the invention of a phonetic alphabet, and the use of writing in literary composition. Here civilization begins. This leaves in the Upper Status, for example, the Grecian tribes of the Homeric age, the Italian tribes shortly before the founding of Rome, and the Germanic tribes of the time of Caesar.

VII. *Status of Civilization.* It commenced, as stated, with the use of a phonetic alphabet and the production of literary records, and divides into *Ancient* and *Modern*. As an equivalent, hieroglyphical writing upon stone may be admitted.

Recapitulation

Periods	*Conditions*
I. Older Period of Savagery	I. Lower Status of Savagery
II. Middle Period of Savagery	II. Middle Status of Savagery
III. Later Period of Savagery	III. Upper Status of Savagery
IV. Older Period of Barbarism	IV. Lower Status of Barbarism
V. Middle Period of Barbarism	V. Middle Status of Barbarism

VI. Later Period of Barbarism   VI. Upper Status of Barbarism
                        VII. Status of Civilization

I. *Lower Status of Savagery,* from the infancy of the human race to the commencement of the next period.

II. *Middle Status of Savagery,* from the acquisition of a fish subsistence and a knowledge of the use of fire, to etc.

III. *Upper Status of Savagery,* from the invention of the bow and arrow, to etc.

IV. *Lower Status of Barbarism,* from the invention of the art of pottery, to etc.

V. *Middle Status of Barbarism,* from the domestication of animals on the Eastern hemisphere, and in the Western from the cultivation of maize and plants by irrigation, with the use of adobe-brick and stone, to etc.

VI. *Upper Status of Barbarism,* from the invention of the process of smelting iron ore, with the use of iron tools, to etc.

VII. *Status of Civilization,* from the invention of a phonetic alphabet, with the use of writing, to the present time.

Each of these periods has a distinct culture and exhibits a mode of life more or less special and peculiar to itself. This specialization of ethnical periods renders it possible to treat a particular society according to its condition of relative advancement, and to make it a subject of independent study and discussion. It does not affect the main result that different tribes and nations on the same continent, and even of the same linguistic family, are in different conditions at the same time, since for our purpose the *condition* of each is the material fact, the *time* being immaterial. . . .

In studying the condition of tribes and nations in these several ethnical periods we are dealing, substantially, with the ancient history and condition of our own remote ancestors.

Richard Whately

A CREATIONIST'S VIEW OF THE ADVENT OF CIVILIZATION

The creationist's view of the advent of civilization is diametrically opposed to that of the evolutionist. In the nineteenth century, Archbishop Richard Whately argued in his Introductory Lectures on Political Economy *(1831) that no evidence could be garnered to support the view that man had advanced, unaided, from the level of savagery to civilization. Man was created civilized and savages are simply examples of civilized men in a degenerate state. This degenerate state was never universal. That mankind could not have civilized himself is proof of the agency of a divine Creator. Whately, an Oxford graduate, became Drummond Professor of Political Economy at Oxford in 1829 and resigned the position in 1831 on his advancement to the archiepiscopal see of Dublin.*

Lecture V

Whether mankind have emerged from the savage state. It was observed in the last Lecture, that civilized Man has not emerged from the savage state;—that the progress of any community in civilization, by its own internal means, must always have begun from a condition removed from that of complete barbarism; out of which it does not appear that men ever did or can raise themselves.

This assertion is at variance with the hypothesis apparently laid down by several writers on Political-Economy; who have described the case of a supposed race of savages, subsisting on the spontaneous productions of the earth, and the precarious supplies of hunting and fishing; and have then traced the steps by which the various arts of life would gradually have arisen, and advanced more and more towards perfection.

One man, it is supposed, having acquired more skill than his neighbors in the making of bows and arrows, or darts, would find it advantageous both for them and for himself, to devote himself to this manufacture, and to exchange these implements for the food procured by others, instead of employing himself in the pursuit of game. Another, from a similar cause, would occupy himself exclusively in the construction of huts, or of canoes; another, in the pre-

Reprinted from Richard Whately, *Introductory Lectures on Political Economy* (2nd ed.; London: B. Fellows, 1832), pp. 108–127.

paring of skins for clothing, etc. And the division of labor having thus begun, the advantages of it would be so apparent, that it would rapidly be extended, and would occasion each person to introduce improvements into the art to which he would have chiefly confined his attention. Those who had studied the haunts and the habits of certain kinds of wild animals, and had made a trade of supplying the community with them, would be led to domesticate such species as were adapted for it, in order to secure a supply of provisions, when the chase might prove insufficient. Those who had especially studied the places of growth, and times of ripening, of such wild fruits, or other vegetable productions, as were in request, would be induced to secure themselves a readier supply, by cultivating them in suitable spots. And thus the Society being divided into Husbandmen, Shepherds, and Artificers of various kinds, exchanging the produce of their various labors, would advance, with more or less steadiness and rapidity, towards the higher stages of civilization.

I have spoken of this description as being conformable to the views *apparently* entertained by some writers, and I have said, "apparently," because I doubt whether it is fair to conclude, that all, or any of them, have designed to maintain that this, or something similar, is a correct account of a matter of fact;—that mankind universally, or some portions of them, have *actually* emerged, by such a process, from a state of complete barbarism. Some may have believed this; but others may have meant merely that it is *possible,* without contending that it has ever in fact occurred; and others again may have not even gone so far as this, but may have intended merely to describe the *steps by which* such a change must take place, supposing it ever *could* occur.

Be this as it may, when we dismiss for a moment all antecedent conjectures, and look around us for instances, we find, I think I may confidently affirm, no one recorded, of a tribe of savages, properly so styled, rising into a civilized state, without instruction and assistance from people already civilized. And we *have,* on the other hand, accounts of various savage tribes, in different parts of the globe, who have been visited from time to time at considerable intervals, but have had no settled intercourse with civilized people, and who appear to continue, as far as can be ascertained, in the same uncultivated condition.

It will probably have occurred to most of you, that the earliest historical records that exist, represent mankind as originally existing in a state far superior to that of our supposed savages. The Book of Genesis describes Man as not having been, like the brutes, created, and then left to provide for himself by his innate bodily and mental faculties, but as having received, in the first instance, immediate divine instructions and communications: and so early, according to this account, was the *division of labor,* that of the first two men who were born of woman, the one was a keeper of cattle, and the other a tiller of the ground.

Scripture not to be referred to in the outset, in examining the question. If this account be received, it must be admitted, that all savages must originally have degenerated from a more civilized state of existence. But I am particularly anxious to point out, that, in a question of this kind, I think it best that the Scriptures should not be appealed to, in the first instance, as a work of *inspiration,* but (if at all) simply as an *historical record* of acknowledged antiquity. And in the present instance I am the more desirous of observing this caution, because I think that the inquiry now before us, if conducted with a reference to no authority but those of reason and experience, will lead to a result which furnishes a very powerful confirmation of the truth of our religion: and it is plain that this evidence would be destroyed by an appeal to the authority of Scripture in the outset; which would of course be a *petitio principii.*

It should be observed, moreover, that the hypothesis above alluded to is not necessarily at variance with the historical records of the creation and earliest condition of mankind. These do indeed declare, that mankind did not begin to exist in the savage state; but it would not thence follow, that a nation which had subsequently sunk into that state, might not raise itself again out of this barbarism.

Historical evidence on the negative side. Such, however, does not appear to be the fact. On looking around us and examining all history, ancient and modern, we find, as I have said, that no savage tribe appears to have risen into civilization, except through the aid of others who were civilized. We have, I think, in this case all the historical evidence that a *negative* is susceptible of; viz. we have the knowledge of numerous cases in which such a change has *not* taken place, and of none where it has; while we have every reason to expect, that, if it had occurred, it would have been recorded.

On this subject I will take the liberty of citing a passage from a very well-written and instructive book, the account of the New Zealanders, in the Library of Entertaining Knowledge; a passage, which is the more valuable to our present purpose, inasmuch as the writer is not treating of the subject with any view whatever to the evidences of religion, and is apparently quite unconscious of the argument which (as I shall presently show) may be deduced from what he says.

> The especial distinction of the savage, and that which, more than any other thing, keeps him a savage, is his ignorance of letters. This places the community almost in the same situation with a herd of the lower animals, insofar as the accumulation of knowledge, or, in other words, any kind of movement forward, is concerned; for it is only by means of the art of writing, that the knowledge acquired by the experience of one generation can be properly stored up, so that none of it shall be lost, for the use of all that are to follow. Among savages, for want of this admirable method of preservation, there is reason to believe the fund of knowledge possessed by the community instead of growing, generally diminishes with time. If we except the absolutely necessary arts of life, which are in daily use and cannot be forgotten, the existing generation seldom seems to possess anything derived from the past. Hence, the oldest man of the tribe is always looked up to as the wisest; simply because he has lived the longest; it being felt that an individual has scarcely a chance of knowing anything more than his own experience has taught him. Accordingly the New Zealanders, for example, seem to have been *in quite as advanced a state when Tasman discovered the country in* 1642, *as they were when Cook visited it,* 127 *years after.*

It may be remarked, however, with reference to this statement, that the absence of written records is, though a very important, rather a secondary than a primary obstacle. It is one branch of that general characteristic of the savage, *improvidence.* If you suppose the case of a savage taught to read and write, but allowed to remain, in all other respects, the same careless, thoughtless kind of Being, and afterwards left to himself, he would most likely forget his acquisition; and would certainly, by neglecting to teach it to his children, suffer it to be lost in the next generation. On the other hand, if you conceive such a case (which certainly is conceivable, and I am disposed to think it a real one) as that of a people ignorant of this art, but acquiring in some degree a thoughtful and provident character, I have little doubt that their desire, thence arising, to record permanently their laws, practical maxims, and discoveries, would gradually lead them, first to the use of memorial-verses, and afterwards to some kind of material symbols, such as picture-writing, and then hieroglyphics; which might gradually be still further improved into writing properly so called.

There are several circumstances which have conduced to keep out of sight the important fact I have been alluding to. The chief of these probably is, the vagueness with which the term "Savage" is applied. I do not profess, and indeed it is evidently not possible, to draw a line by which we may determine precisely to whom that title is, and is not, applicable; since there is a series of almost insensible gradations between the highest and the lowest state of human society. Nor is any such exact boundary-line needed for our present purpose. It is sufficient if we admit, what is probably very far short of the truth, that those who are in as *low a state as some tribes with which we are acquainted,* are incapable of emerging from it, by their own unassisted efforts. But many probably are misled by the language of the Greeks and Romans, who called all men barbarians except themselves. Many, and perhaps all other nations, fell short of *them* in civilization: but several nations, even among the less cultivated of the ancient barbarians, were very far removed from what we should be understood to mean by the savage state, and which is to be found among many tribes at the present day. For instance, the ancient Germans were probably as much elevated above that state, as we are above theirs. A people who cultivated corn, though their agriculture was probably in a very rude state—who not only had numerous herds of cattle, but employed the labor of brutes, and even made use of cavalry in their wars, and who also were accustomed to the working of metals, though their supply of them, according to Tacitus, was but scanty—these cannot with propriety be reckoned savages. Or if they are to be so called (for it is not worthwhile to dispute about a word), then I would admit, that, in this sense, men may advance, and in fact have advanced, by their own unassisted efforts, from the savage to the civilized state.

Again, we are liable to be misled by loose and inaccurate descriptions of extensive districts inhabited by distinct tribes of people, differing widely from each other in their degrees of cultivation. Some, for instance, are accustomed to speak of the ancient Britons, in the mass; without considering, that in all probability some of these tribes were nearly as much behind others in civilization, as the Children of the Mist described by Sir Walter Scott in the Legend of Montrose, if compared with the inhabitants of Edinburgh at the same period. And thus it is probable that travelers have represented some nation as in the condition of mere savages, from having viewed only some part of it, or perhaps even some different nation, inhabiting some one district of the country.

When due allowance has been made for these and other sources of inaccuracy, there will be no reason, I think, for believing, that there is any exception to the positions I have here laid down: the impossibility of men's emerging unaided from a completely savage state; and, consequently, the descent of such as are in that state (supposing mankind to have sprung from a single pair) from ancestors less barbarous, and from whom they have degenerated.

Records of this descent, and of this degeneracy, it is, from the nature of the case, not likely we should possess; but several indications of the fact may often be found among savage nations. Some have even traditions to that effect; and almost all possess some one or two arts not of a piece with their general rudeness, and which plainly appear to be remnants of a different state of things; being such, that the first *invention* of them implies a degree of ingenuity beyond what the savages, who *retain* those arts, now possess.

It is very interesting to look over the many copious accounts we possess of various savage tribes, with a view to this point. You will find, I think, in the course of such an inquiry, that each savage tribe having retained such arts as are most essential to their subsistence in the particular country in which they are placed, there is accordingly, generally speaking, somewhat less of degeneracy in many points, in the colder climates; because these will not admit of the same degree of that characteristic of savages, improvidence. Such negligence in providing clothing and habitations, and in laying up stores of provisions, as, in warm and fertile countries, is not incompatible with subsistence in a very rude state, would, in more inhospitable regions, destroy the whole race in the course of a single winter.

Causes of degeneracy into barbarism. As to the causes which have occasioned any portions of mankind thus to degenerate, we are, of course, in most instances, left to mere conjecture: but there seems little reason to doubt, that the principal cause has been War.

A people perpetually harassed by predatory hostile incursions, and still more, one compelled to fly their country and take refuge in mountains or forests,[1] or to wander to some distant unoccupied region (and this we know to have been anciently a common occurrence) must of course be likely to sink in point of civilization. They must, amidst a series of painful struggles for mere existence, have their attention drawn off from all other subjects; they must be deprived of the materials and the opportunities for practicing many of the arts, till the knowledge of them is lost; and their children must grow up, in each successive generation, more and more uninstructed, and disposed to be satisfied with a life approaching to that of the brutes.

A melancholy picture of the operation of these causes is presented in the kingdom of Abyssinia; which seems to have been for a considerable time verging more and more, from a state of comparative civilization, towards barbarism, through the incessant hostile incursions of its Pagan neighbors, the Galla.

But whatever may have been the causes which in each instance have tended to barbarize each nation, of this we may, I think, be well assured, that though, if it have not sunk below a certain point, it may, under favorable circumstances, be expected to rise again, and gradually even more than recover the lost ground; on the other hand, there is a stage of degradation from which it *cannot* emerge, but through the means of intercourse with some more civilized people. The turbulent and unrestrained passions—the indolence—and, above all, the want of forethought, which are characteristic of savages, naturally tend to prevent, and, as experience seems to show, always have prevented, that process of gradual advancement from taking place, which was sketched out in the opening of this Lecture; except when the savage is stimulated by the example, and supported by the guidance and instruction, of men superior to himself.

Anyone who dislikes the conclusions to which these views lead, will probably set himself to contend against the *arguments* which prove it *unlikely* that savages should civilize themselves; but how will he get over the *fact,* that they never yet *have* done this? That they never *can,* is a theory; and something may always be said, well or ill, against any theory; but facts are stubborn things; and that no

[1] Whence the name "Savage," *Silvagio.*

authenticated instance can be produced of savages that ever *did* emerge unaided from that state, is no *theory,* but a statement, hitherto uncontradicted, of a matter of *fact.*

Confirmation of Scripture-history from existing monuments. Now if this be the case, when, and how, did civilization first *begin?* If Man when first created was left, like the brutes, to the unaided exercise of his natural powers of body and mind—those powers which are common to the European and to the New-Hollander[2]—how comes it that the European is not now in the condition of the New-Hollander? As the soil itself and the climate of New-Holland are excellently adapted to the growth of corn, and yet (as corn is not indigenous there) could never have borne any, to the end of the world, if it had not been brought thither from another country, and sown; so, the savage himself, though he may be, as it were, a soil capable of receiving the seeds of civilization, can never, in the first instance, produce it, as of spontaneous growth; and unless those seeds be introduced from some other quarter, must remain forever in the sterility of barbarism. And from what quarter then could this first beginning of civilization have been supplied, to the earliest race of mankind? According to the present course of nature, the first introducer of cultivation among savages, is, and must be, Man, in a more improved state: in the beginning therefore of the human race, this, since there was no *man* to effect it, must have been the work of *another Being.* There must have been, in short, a *Revelation* made, to the first, or to some subsequent generation, of our species. And this miracle (for such it is, as being an impossibility according to the present course of nature) is attested, *independently* of the authority of Scripture, and consequently in *confirmation* of the Scripture-accounts, by the fact, that civilized Man exists at the present day.

Taking this view of the subject, we have no need to dwell on the utility—the importance—the antecedent probability—of a Revelation: it is established as a fact, of which a monument is existing before our eyes. Divine instruction is proved to be necessary, not merely for an end which *we think desirable,* or which *we think* agreeable to Divine wisdom and goodness, but, for an end which we *know has been* attained. That Man could not have *made* himself, is appealed to as a proof of the agency of a divine *Creator:* and that Mankind

---

[2] Australia was formerly called New-Holland.—Ed.

could not in the first instance have *civilized* themselves, is a proof, exactly of the same kind, and of equal strength, of the agency of a divine *Instructor.*

You will, I suspect, find this argument press so hard on the adversaries of religion, that they will be not unlikely to attempt evading its force, by calling on you to produce an instance of some one art, *peculiar to civilized* men, and which it may be proved could not have been derived but from inspiration. But this is a manifest evasion of the argument. For, so far from representing as *peculiar* to *civilized* men all arts that seem beyond the power of savages to *invent,* I have remarked the *direct contrary:* which indeed is just what might have been expected, supposing savages to be, as I have contended, in a *degenerated* state.

The argument really employed (and all attempts to misrepresent it are but fresh presumptions that it is unanswerable) consists in an appeal, not to any *particular art* or arts, but to a *civilized condition,* generally. If this was *not* the work of a divine instructor, *produce an instance,* if you can, of a nation of savages *who have civilized themselves!*

Such is the evidence which an attentive survey of human transactions will supply, to those who do not, in their too hasty zeal, begin by appealing to the authority of Scripture in matters which we are competent to investigate.

The full development of this branch of evidence, which I have slightly noticed, but which it would be unsuitable to the character of these Lectures to enlarge on, will be found, I think, to lead to very interesting and important views.

Mankind then having, as Scripture informs us, been favored from the first with an immediate intercourse with the Creator, and having been placed in a condition, as keepers of domestic animals, and cultivators of the earth, more favorable to the development of the rational faculties, than, we have every reason to think, they could ever have reached by the mere exercise of their natural powers; it is probable they were thenceforth left to themselves in all that relates to the invention and improvement of the arts of life. If we judge from the analogy of the other parts of revelation, we find it agreeable to the general designs of Providence, that such knowledge, and such only, should be imparted to Man *supernaturally,* as he could not *otherwise* have attained; and that whatever he is capable of discovering by the exercise of his natural faculties (however important the knowledge of it may be) he should be left so to discover for himself: —in short, that no further miraculous interference should take place, than is absolutely indispensable. And if again we judge from observation, we know that a knowledge of *all* the arts of life was not divinely communicated. The first race of Mankind seem to have been placed merely in such a state as might enable and incite them to commence, and continue, a course of advancement.

Errors respecting a "state of Nature." And to place Man in such a state, seems in fact no more than analogous to what was done for the lower animals in the mere act of creation, considering how much more completely they are furnished with instincts than we are. To have left man (as the brutes are left) in what is called a state of nature, i.e. in the condition of an adult who should have grown up totally without cultivation, would have been to leave him with his principal faculties not only undeveloped, but without a chance of ever being developed; which is not the case with the brutes. Such a procedure therefore would in reality not have been analogous to what takes place in respect of the lower animals, but would have been disproportionately disadvantageous to man. In fact, there is no good reason for calling the condition of the rudest savages "a state of nature," unless the phrase be used (as perhaps in strictness it ought) to denote merely ignorance of *Arts*. But to call their's a state of Nature (as several writers have done) in the sense of "a natural state," is a use of language as much at variance with sound philosophy, as the dreams of those who imagine this state to resemble the golden age of the poets, are, with well-ascertained facts. The peaceful life and gentle disposition, the freedom from oppression, the exemption from selfishness and from evil passions, and the simplicity of character, of savages, have no existence but in the fictions of poets, and the fancies of vain speculators: nor can their mode of life be called, with any propriety, the natural state of man. A plant would not be said to be in its natural state, which was growing in a soil or climate that precluded it from putting forth the flowers and the fruit for which its organization was destined. No one who saw the pine growing near the boundary of perpetual snow on the Alps, stunted to the height of two or three feet, and struggling to exist amidst rocks and glaciers, would describe that as the natural state of a tree, which in a more genial soil and climate, a little lower down, was found capable of rising to the height of fifty or sixty yards. In like manner, the natural state of man must, according to all fair analogy, be reckoned not that in which his intellectual and moral growth are as it were stunted, and permanently repressed, but one in which his original endowments are, I do not say, brought to perfection, but enabled to exercise themselves, and to expand, like the flowers of a plant; and, especially, in which that characteristic of our species, the tendency towards progressive *improvement,* is permitted to come into play.

Such, then, I say, seems to have been the state in which the earliest race of mankind were placed by the Creator.

II CIVILIZATION: UNILINEAL OR MULTIPLE BEGINNINGS?

G. Elliot Smith

THE CRADLE OF CIVILIZATION: EGYPT

In the decades around the turn of the present century there emerged a school of thought which argued that civilization was never independently acquired by man through a process of evolution, but was spread from one common center via trade, the movement of people, or the clash of culture. The appearance of similar cultural elements in two distant parts of the world should not suggest independent cultural development, but diffusion. Grafton Elliot Smith, the father of British anthropology, reflects the hyperdiffusionist position as he argues for the diffusion of all culture from Egypt. His Egypto-centric hyperdiffusionist doctrine began in 1900, when he became the first occupant of the chair of anatomy in the Government Medical School at Cairo. He was later a professor of anatomy at Manchester and at University College, London. He died in 1937.

The creation of civilization was the most tremendous revolution in the whole course of human history. Within a few centuries so profound a change was effected in the mode of life, the aims and occupations, and in the size of the population and in the areas affected by these changes, as to open a new chapter of Man's career with new standards of values and new social conditions and aspirations.

Civilization is not simply a jumble of new arts and crafts. It is an amazingly complex organization which gave Man an entirely new outlook on the world and his activities in it. It involved a great deal more than the mere invention of even so impressive a list of new occupations as irrigation and agriculture, cattle-breeding and pottery-making, weaving and house-building, working gold and copper, carpentry and stonemasonry, architecture and boat building, the making of clothing and the brewing of beer, the use of arithmetic and the devising of calendars. It was responsible for the origin of the kingship and for conferring upon the king the reputation of being not merely the distributor of the waters of irrigation, but also the actual Giver of Life to the land and to the seed which the inundation made fertile; of being not merely the measurer of the year and the predictor of the time of inundation, but also the actual cause of the inundation and the Creator of the dry land that emerged when the waters subsided. The king was the Giver of Life and the Creator. He was regarded as the source of the life of the whole population and the creator of the State. In a much more absolute sense than was involved in the famous boast of the King of France, the earliest king in the history of the world was regarded as "The State."

When it was discovered, by observation of the heliacal rising of the star Sirius, that the Sun was a more accurate measurer of the year than the moon and, as the early Egyptians thought, also the cause of the inundation, they identified it with the king, who had already been credited with the same functions. The dead king was then believed to pass to the sky and become one with the Sun. This idea of the Sun-God involved the creation of a sky world as the home of dead kings, who attained immortality by becoming identified with the great Giver of Life in the celestial regions. . . .

. . . Before the inauguration of the social system of city life we call civilization, men of different races had been wandering throughout the whole extent of the continental areas of the world. Apart from the making of such simple implements of flint, bone and wood as were necessary for the capture of animals for food or for protecting themselves from wild beasts, these primitive men were devoid of any arts and crafts. They were simply nomads wholly occupied in the pursuit of food and in an unceasing vigil to safeguard their existence. In these pursuits their distinctively human qualities of vision and understanding enabled them to acquire amazing skill and cunning, so that they survived in competition with the greater strength and speed, and the power to inflict damage, possessed by many animals. They led a life of happy innocence. The world was theirs. They had neither houses nor farms to tie them to one place. They had neither clothes nor property to carry about with them. They had no leaders to command their actions or hampering social or political regulations to restrict their freedom.

What then were the circumstances that brought to an end this era of Arcadian simplicity with its "liberty, equality and fraternity," to use the phraseology which the French Humanists of the eighteenth century devised from their study of Natural Man? . . .

Archaeological investigations during the last quarter of a century have thrown enough light upon the conditions that obtained in the world at the beginning of the third millennium B.C. to justify the inference that, excepting in Egypt, Mesopotamia, Western Asia and Crete, the whole world was still in the food-gathering phase. In attempting to arrive at a solution of the much disputed problem as to which of the closely associated peoples, all members of the Mediterranean Race, was the pioneer in creating civilization, we can eliminate Crete, not only because its dependence on Egypt and Western Asia for its cultural capital is generally recognized, but also because it is obvious that until sea-going ships had been invented—and their invention was the work of a people already committed to the regimen of civilization—neither population nor culture could have reached this island in the Mediterranean. With reference to Syria and Western Asia no traces of early culture are known which cannot be referred to the inspiration of Egypt or Mesopotamia. At the moment, therefore, the issue is reduced to the question whether Egypt or Sumer (with Elam) was the pioneer. The essential similarity of the two earliest manifestations of culture-development in these two localities and the identity of their peculiarly distinctive repertory of strange practices allows no room for doubt that, whichever was the pioneer, the other place drew its inspiration from the more precocious inventor.

In 1926 Professor James H. Breasted, having then recently returned from a critical study on the spot of the new archaeological discoveries in Egypt, Syria and Mesopotamia, expressed his opinion in no uncertain voice. In *The Conquest of Civilization* he announced that "it is now a finally established fact that civilization first arose in Egypt." The constant repetition since then by other scholars, of the statement that Sumerian (and Elamite) civilization antedates Egyptian, makes it necessary to emphasize the fact that all the discoveries which have been made in Sumer since 1926 add further corroboration to the accuracy of Professor Breasted's judgment. Taking the dates, which every archaeologist accepts, it is a simple problem in arithmetic to reach the conclusion that civilization was growing and flourishing in Predynastic Egypt at least five centuries before the earliest evidence revealed in Sumer. Moreover, in addition to the unassailable testimony of chronology, it can be demonstrated, as the following pages will show, that the peculiar form early civilization assumed, not only in Egypt but in every part of the

world, was determined in large measure by the practice of mummification on the banks of the Nile in the middle of the fourth millennium B.C.

The ancient tradition of Osiris[1] recorded by Plutarch probably
represents an essentially accurate report of what actually happened
nearly forty centuries before the Greek essayist wrote. "When Osiris
came to his kingdom" he is said by Plutarch to have found "the Egyptians living a life such as animals lead. He taught them the art of agriculture, gave them laws and instructed them in the worship of the
gods. Then he traversed the whole world on a mission of civilization."
Archaeological research has revealed the fact that Egyptian civilization is vastly older than that of any other part of the world, and the
form this earliest civilization assumed affords a complete demonstra-
tion of the fact that it was actually created on the banks of the Nile. In
the following pages the evidence in substantiation of this claim will
be set forth. Hence Plutarch is probably right in claiming that Egypt's
first king found his subjects "living a life such as animals live." For
if the Egyptians created civilization they must have been living the
life of Natural Man before they began their pioneer work. Osiris also
devised the art of agriculture, created the State System, and was the
first god of whom antiquity has preserved any record. Though it is
unlikely that Osiris himself traveled abroad there is no doubt that
his works "traversed the whole world on a mission of civilization."
Plutarch had clearly rescued an ancient tradition in which was crys-
talized the true story of the origin of civilization.

When for the first time in the history of the world the group of
people who happened to be living in Egypt abandoned the nomadic
life and began to till the soil, they were accomplishing a vastly
greater revolution in the affairs of mankind than the mere invention
of the crafts of the farmer and the irrigation engineer. They were
committing themselves to the much more formidable task of erecting
the complicated edifice of civilization and formulating the fantastic
doctrine of the State System which has dominated the world ever
since. The creation of the State involved not only the invention of a
multitude of arts and crafts, but also a complicated social and political organization under the rulership of a king endowed with peculiar powers and an authority over the lives of his subjects and the

---

[1] In Egyptian mythology, Osiris was the god of the dead and of life after death. He
was also the father of agriculture and civilization.—Ed.

control of his kingdom, which was believed to be, in the fullest sense of the word, absolute. The identification of the State with the life of one man, making the welfare of the whole community and every individual citizen utterly dependent upon his ability to perform certain ritual acts, is the amazing phenomenon we have to study and, if possible, explain.

The natural crop of barley, which was growing wild on the banks of the Nile, seems to have provided the lure to attract the earliest settlers in Egypt. As the population increased and a more abundant supply of grain was needed, some man of exceptional insight imitated the natural processes, which people had probably been witnessing for untold generations. He dug channels to allow the innundation to extend more widely. Hence arose the system of basin irrigation and with it the beginning of agriculture. Baskets and pottery were devised to hold the seed, and granaries were invented to store it—which may have suggested to men the possibility of erecting houses to protect themselves also, one of those apparently obvious things Natural Man had neglected to do. Incidentally the makers of baskets and matting discovered that they could make a much finer "matting" from the flax growing in their fields. Thus they invented the spinning and weaving of linen.

The vital importance of irrigation compelled the Egyptians to study the habits of the river, to measure its rise and fall, to count the days that intervened between the inundations—in other words to invent arithmetic and devise a calendar. The yearly measurement of time, which originally was made by observations of the river, involved complicated calculations. But time was also being measured by the more easily calculated periods, the months which the phases of the moon determined. The similarity of these cyclical changes with the physiological periodicity of women suggested the belief that there was a causal relationship—that the moon was controlling the lives of individuals upon the earth, and in particular the life-producing functions of womankind. This conception of a celestial influence over mundane affairs was strengthened when it was realized that Sirius, one of the seven stars in the constellation known to modern astronomers as Canis Major, after being invisible from the beginning of June, reappeared in the east a few minutes before sunrise in July, exactly at the time when the Nile flood began in Middle Egypt. This coincidence of course applies only to one particular circumstance and one particular place. Hence it affords decisive evidence upon the question of the place of origin. The inundation of the Nile was the most vital and impressive natural phenomenon in Egypt. It provided an assurance of food and prosperity for the whole community and every individual. The coincidence of the rising of Sirius with the inundation was believed by the Egyptians to have the relation of cause and effect. Hence it played an essential part, not merely in corroborating the hypothesis of celestial control of human affairs, which the moon's cycles had previously suggested, but also in helping to build up a comprehensive theory of the regulation by the sky of all really vital affairs of the earth. This archaic form of astrology was destined to exert a far-reaching influence upon thought and speculation for the next sixty centuries. It played a tremendous part in provoking the enquiries out of which eventually emerged our conception of the universe.

Several centuries after the first measurement of the year in Egypt the growth of astronomical knowledge led some man of conspicuous ability to suggest the replacement of the old calendar, based upon observations of the river, by a new calendar determined by observations on the sun and Sirius. In the world of belief this application of astronomical knowledge was responsible for transferring the home of the dead from the earth to the sky, and for emphasizing the solar attributes of the king-god. Hence the Sun-God Re seemed to usurp the place of the River-God Osiris. It is probable however that, contrary to the views now current, the Egyptians had only one god, whose river-controlling powers were at first most abstrusive (namely Osiris the Giver of Life and Measurer of the Year by the river), and later, when the solar attributes were emphasized, the same god was called Re (who in the form of the sun measured the year).

The tremendous influence of the belief in a Sun-God on the development of human thought and belief, as well as of social practices, is one of the cardinal facts in the history of the world. In the light of the considerations set forth in the preceding pages it is certain that the invention of the Solar Calendar and the creation of the Sun-God occurred at Heliopolis.

Thus the simple fact that in Egypt men began to practice irrigation and agriculture led them also to make pottery, granaries, houses and linen, to invent arithmetic and the calendar, to create the kingship, to develop ideas of celestial control of human destiny and of such mundane affairs as affect Man's welfare, and to create a Sun-God. But a host of other significant results followed in the train of these momentous events. . . .

In many other ways the adoption of agriculture transformed the conditions of life. The rapid accumulation of population in a narrow valley that was flooded every year necessarily involved the concentration of the dwelling houses on those isolated elevations that rose above the level of the inundation. Hence communities became herded together in villages and people were forced into more intimate association than they had experienced during their career as nomads.

The creation of the village was a momentous event in Human History. Not only did it determine the conditions that are implicit in the literal meaning of the word civilization and compel Man for the first time to devise a social organization, but in addition the circumstances under which it developed promoted certain incidental results of far-reaching influence upon the subsequent history of mankind. . . .

The cultivation of the soil and the congregation of people in villages were responsible for profound changes in the treatment of the dead.

Primitive Man had been in the habit of leaving his dead wherever they happened to die. The new circumstances that developed among the Food-Producers made it incumbent on him to bury his dead and to make cemeteries beyond the limit of the cultivated area in the sand of the desert. This practice led to surprising results which were in large measure responsible for shaping the subsequent history of civilization.

The burial of the dead in the hot dry sand was often followed by the desiccation of the body, which became exempt from the forces of corruption. This natural preservation of the body was made known to the living by the depredations of jackals. The early Egyptians were thus led to associate this phenomenon with these carnivores and also to devote much more attention to the corpses of the dead than they had formerly received. If we may judge from the writings of Egyptians several centuries later, or, what is more important, their immediate reaction to the wonder of desiccation, we can be confident that they regarded the preservation of the body as an obvious token of the prolongation of the deceased's existence. As the body was not destroyed neither was the deceased man's (or woman's) existence at an end.

Whether this is the true interpretation or not, the graves themselves provide definite evidence that increasing attention was devoted to the care of the corpse during the Predynastic period. It was wrapped in linen, and around the swathed body the skin of an ox or goat was wrapped to protect it from contact with the soil. Implements, ornaments, and other precious objects, as well as food, were put in the grave.

As this provision for the deceased's comfort and welfare became more lavish the size of the grave increased to accomodate the growing needs, and produced a series of experiments in grave construction, which produced very important results—the invention of brick-making, carpentry, stone-working, and mummification, the evolution of architecture, and the vast revolution in thought and speculation that emerged from the belief that the mummies were not merely spared the fate of corruption but could be reanimated to continue living. . . .

True civilization began when Man adopted a settled mode of life based upon the practice of agriculture. The realization of the possibility of obtaining a secure means of sustenance without giving up his whole time to the daily search for food induced Man to settle in a definite place, which he made his home. It also provided him with the leisure and the inducement to devise arts and crafts and a social organization the lack of which was not felt by simple nomads.

At first sight it might seem highly improbable that Man began agriculture as an irrigator. Nevertheless it is true that the first traces of civilization are found in two practically rainless regions, Egypt and Sumer. With the recent laying bare of the foundations of history as distinguished from tradition, it seems certain that the Egyptian civilization was evolved in the valley of the Nile, and equally certain that the germs of Sumerian and Babylonian civilization were imported. In the Nile Valley every phase may be followed, from simple nomadism to the highest culture, and this without a break. It is idle, therefore, to turn to some hypothetical land, as so many writers are doing today, and assume that the Egyptians acquired their cereals and their knowledge of agriculture from elsewhere, and adapted this knowledge to irrigation in order to meet the new and quite unique conditions of the Nile. Nor is it likely that Man cultivated the vine and olive first, and subsequently applied this hypothetical experience of agriculture to the cereals. As a matter of fact, the two oldest civilizations, Egypt and Elam-Sumer, depended entirely on irrigation, while the second group, which clustered round these—Assyria, Persia, Phoenicia and Syria—were all noted for their skill in irrigation. The earliest known people of Indo-European speech—the Kassites and Mitanni—appear to have had no culture before they came into contact with the civilization of the Ancient East. It may also be something more than a coincidence that the Hittites arose on the edge of the salt treeless tract in Central Asia Minor. In this district irrigation for summer crops is now practiced. The Hittites may also have been acquainted with the art.

In the history of mankind there is a mystery that is insoluble unless we assume that the Egyptians were in reality the first of mankind to cultivate cereals. . . .

If we assume for the moment that barley and millet were found growing wild, the art of cultivation may have been learned in Egypt from the simple experiment of imitating on one part of the flood plain what was done naturally by the river. The people saw that wherever the waters of the inundation spread the soil become fertile. Irrigation began by imitating the natural process: scooping out channels to extend the area flooded. Throughout all the area of the valley under flood there were in Egypt unique features *such as are not found elsewhere in the world.* The most important of these was the seasonal incidence of the floods. The plain was soaked at the very end of the hot season, so that the land remained moist for several months. During the cool season evaporation was small compared with what it would have been if the flood had come at the beginning of the summer. The slope of the plain was such that very large areas were soon clear of the water. Stagnant swamps were not a great feature of the valley. At the same time the temperature in the cool season was high enough to keep millet, barley, and flax steadily growing until the opening of the following summer. . . .

The plants appear above the ground a few days after the water drains off, and ripen at the beginning of the hot season, before the soil is parched by the oncoming summer. The seeds lie on the surface of the land without injury until next flood season, when it is again soaked and the cycle begins anew. These unique circumstances, combined with the knowledge that barley was the staple food of the earliest Egyptians, force us to conclude that the Egyptians must have been the inventors of the art of agriculture. . . .

Thus, to repeat and reemphasize the fact, the most momentous event in human history occurred when some man first scooped shallow channels to extend the area of inundation. Experience would soon lead to the closing or deepening of these first channels at given periods, and so the first steps towards "basin irrigation" would be made. In basin irrigation the flood water is led in this way from the first to a number of other level areas in succession, the necessary works in the shape of channels and banks being small affairs. The surface of the flood plain needed no leveling or adjustment to prepare the way for effective irrigation. The tops of the banks have become the pathways from village to village. . . .

The first steps towards agriculture were thus very simple in some parts, at least, of the Nile Valley. Subsequently larger banks would be made and channels dug to control the water, and by the primitive *shadouf* the water could be lifted from the river or channel in order to help the crops in parts which appeared to be too dry.

Irrigation was thus made perennial by a simple and natural course of development. That this was the real order of events is confirmed by the earliest beliefs of the Egyptian people—the ideas which became the foundation of their religion. An obvious scientific explanation is forthcoming if we assume that the order of events was: first, the use of wild millet and barley and the gathering and storing of the seeds: second, the use of sticks to till the land, combined with simple improvements in the method of regulating the flooding and drainage of the land, in other words, imitating the natural basin irrigation: third, transforming backwaters and lagoons into canals from which the water was lifted into small channels by the *shadouf*.

The conditions that have always existed in Egypt are paralleled by those of no other river in the world. The other rivers on the banks of which high civilizations have arisen are the Euphrates and Tigris, the Indus and Ganges, and the great rivers of China. In all these cases irrigation is practiced, but not in the way that is normal in Egypt.

In Mesopotamia, the flood reaches its maximum at the end of May, and the rivers are again within their banks in June. But this is full summer, and plants that appear after the flood has left the plain have no chance of reaching maturity. The soil dries so rapidly that the mud is replaced by dust in the course of a few days. The flood is caused chiefly by the melting of the snow on the mountains of Armenia, which, of course, begins with the return of late spring. The plain of Mesopotamia is rainless in summer, so that the dry mud remains a barren waste. The few showers that mark each year occur in midwinter. These floods, therefore, require regulating before the water can be used for profitable irrigation, for the single application of water, which comes naturally each year, is not capable of bringing any crop to maturity. As Sir Hanbury Brown has pointed out: "under the extreme conditions of heat and dryness, which prevail in summer, it would be lost labor to sow seed, which, though it might germinate, would wither away before coming to maturity."

These circumstances in Mesopotamia must be borne in mind, because they are all-important in their bearing on the question of the priority of Egyptian or Sumerian civilization, as well as on the still more fundamental question of the most probable localities for the evolution of barley and wheat before Man interfered with the process. From these considerations it is clear that the Sumerians must have learned from the Egyptians how to use the river water for irrigation.

In India, the two great rivers are fed from the snows of the northern mountains, and the floods come early in summer, so that conditions there are similar to those of Mesopotamia. In China, the floods are caused chiefly by the heavy local rains, which occur during the summer months. Thus the incidence of the flood season is all in favor of Egypt as the place where the art of irrigation originated. It is the only land where the annual flood produces crops without any assistance. On the Euphrates, the preliminary requisites are an embankment to keep off the flood and a canal to bring the water from the river at the proper time of year. It is unlikely that such technical knowledge was acquired without the help of the natural object-lesson which the Nile alone provided. . . .

Agriculture is like the use of fire—the invention was a sudden inspiration and not the result of a gradual change. There is no halfway house. A people either tills the soil or it does not, and if it cultivated anything in the Ancient East we may be sure that it knew something of wheat or barley. The limited amount of time that is available for the spread of this knowledge all round the world is forgotten, and was not known to earlier writers on the subject. Because

Man of the Old Stone Age lived apparently as a nonprogressive being, perhaps for hundreds of thousands of years, it was assumed that
civilization took a correspondingly long period to evolve. But, by accepting the modern dates for the beginning of progress in Egypt,
and by recognizing the evidence of the spread of culture, we are
able to see the history of mankind as a consistent whole. Thousands
of years may no longer be evoked to suit the theory of the historian,
for the evolution of civilization in Egypt covered less than the single
millennium which fell between 4000 and 3000 B.C.

If this is the true account of the history of barley, the origin of
civilization was due to the accidental discovery of valuable food
plants growing in the Nile Valley. Man did not deliberately set to
work to solve the problem of becoming a tiller of the soil, but discovered the possibility of cultivation accidentally and without effort.
He helped the river to do the business just a little better than it had
been doing it before his advent. Of his early plants, wild millet is
easily able to hold its own in the valley, but barley had not a very
great margin for safety. Wheat can be best accounted for by its evolution on a small island in the Aegean Archipelago. Here it was found
by men who had already learned from their experience in Egypt how
to cultivate millet and barley.

Perhaps the most remarkable fact of all this story is that Man
should have discovered so many plants, animals and metals of special importance at the dawn of civilization in Egypt. Many of these are
still the most important factors in the economic and industrial life
of modern men, and they have not been superseded by newer products from other parts of the world. In the course of the next thousand
years after agriculture was invented, when Syria, Asia Minor and
Mesopotamia had been added to the domain of the civilized world,
and silver, iron, fruit trees, cotton, the camel and the horse added to
Man's equipment, it may be said that the list of essential raw products was almost complete. Before the epoch 4000 B.C. Man had
hardly begun to appreciate the world's resources; soon after the year
2000 he had gained most of what the earth affords. . . .

. . . In Egypt alone the climatic conditions and the seasons of the
inundation are favorable for the natural growth of barley: and we
know that it was the staple diet of the earliest Egyptians. The climatic conditions in Mesopotamia, Syria and Asia Minor are such
that the cultivation of barley became possible there only when men

applied the lessons of artificial irrigation which they had learned in Egypt. Dr. Cherry[2] believes that wheat must have grown naturally on some of the smaller Aegean Islands—he suggested Melos or Naxos —and was first cultivated centuries after barley, and by men who had learned the art of agriculture directly or indirectly from Egypt. But before the close of the fourth millennium the Egyptian technique of agriculture and irrigation had been adopted in Sumer and probably also in Crete, Syria and Asia Minor. Soon afterwards it was to spread north from Sumer and Elam to Turkestan and east to Baluchistan and the Valley of the Indus. But it probably took another millennium before it spread in Europe as one of the distinctive features of the Neolithic culture there.

[2] Reference is to Professor Thomas Cherry of the University of Melbourne, who published a detailed report in 1921 on the agricultural development in early Egypt. —Ed.

Lord Raglan
THE CRADLE OF CIVILIZATION: MESOPOTAMIA

The hyperdiffusionists generally agree that civilization sprang from one common center, but their unanimity does not carry over into the selection of a site. While Elliot Smith and his followers opted for Egypt, Lord Raglan placed the fountainhead of civilization on the Tigris-Euphrates. Raglan argued that many of the principal aspects of all civilizations could be traced to the early Sumerian settlement near the head of the Persian Gulf. Lord Raglan, in keeping with familial tradition, was educated at the Royal Military College, Sandhurst, and prepared for a military career. His views on the advent of civilization appear to have been stimulated and influenced by his years of military service in various parts of the Near East. In addition to How Came Civilization? *(1939), he published a number of articles on anthropological subjects.*

The purpose of this book is to challenge certain widely held beliefs concerning culture, civilization, and progress, and since we cannot avoid using these frequently ill-used words we must start by attempting to define them. Let us start with culture. A common use of the word is to describe that which distinguishes the educated among us from the uneducated; in this book, however, it will be used in its more strictly scientific sense of patterned behavior, that is to say, behavior which is actuated not by innate impulses but by that which the individual learns, either by instruction or imitation, from other members of his social group. It consists, in fact, of all forms of human behavior, except those which are also found among the apes. The only exceptions are the recent products of original genius, which since they have yet to become patterned, can hardly be considered as expressions of culture. They are, as we shall see later, extremely rare.

There is one element of culture which distinguishes all men from all animals, and that is the use of language. Language is the expression of definite ideas by means of the larynx, lips, and tongue. Apes and other animals can express certain emotions by means of sounds, but attempts to show that these sounds mean something more defi-

From Lord Raglan, *How Came Civilization?* (London: Methuen & Co. Ltd., 1939). Reprinted by permission.

nite have failed. . . . And what is civilization? It may be defined as literate culture. The gulf that divides a literate from an illiterate society is a wide one. Its width is seldom realized, since between literate and illiterate *individuals* there need be no gulf at all. Many illiterates are people of high intelligence, and the plowman or bricklayer who can read just enough to gather the football results from a newspaper may be in no way superior to one who cannot read at all. But a civilized society, insofar as it is civilized, does not consist of plowmen and bricklayers, any more than it consists of foxhunters or politicians. All these occupations may exist in illiterate, that is uncivilized, societies. The persons who follow these occupations may be civilized, but that is another matter. A society is civilized only if it contains scholars and scientists. The scholar consolidates and clarifies the knowledge which has already been acquired, and hands it on to the scientist, who, thus provided, proceeds to experiment, and thus to the increase of knowledge. Without the torch of learning, the scientist is reduced to groping in the dark, and without the scientist to use and test the results of his learning, the scholar sinks into a barren pedantry. Thus scholarship and science, in the widest sense of these terms, are the warp and woof of civilization. And the scientist, no less than the scholar, is dependent upon the written word; not only must he be able to use the learning of the scholars, but he must be able to record the results of his own investigations.

Since, then, civilization depends upon scholarship and science, and these depend upon writing, civilization can only arise where the art of writing is known. Now there are two kinds of writing, the pictorial and the alphabetic. The latter is known to be comparatively modern. Every alphabet in the world is derived from the alphabet which was developed, about the middle of the second millennium B.C., in the Eastern Mediterranean, probably in Phoenicia. This fact, which is undisputed, suggests two conclusions. The first is that since the chief medium of civilization, the alphabet, was diffused from one center, civilization itself was diffused from one center. The second is that since the later kind of writing, the alphabet, which is now almost universal, was diffused from one center, the earlier kind of writing, which never had more than a very limited distribution, was probably diffused from one center. This earlier kind of writing differs from the alphabetic in that each sign represents not a sound but an idea. Writing of this kind, except for some survivals such as our numerals, is now confined to Eastern Asia, and at its widest extent was limited to an area stretching from North Africa through Southern and Eastern Asia to Polynesia and Middle America. It was never used in Europe, the inhabitants of which continent were totally ignorant of writing until the alphabet was introduced from the East. Up to 1000 B.C. Europe beyond the Aegean was totally illiterate and therefore totally uncivilized; the Middle East had then been literate and civilized for thousands of years. . . .

It is not many years since the existence of problems of diffusion was first recognized. Up to the end of the last century resemblances in culture were accepted as belonging to one of two classes, those of which the history was known, and those of which the history was unknown. If the history was known, as, for example, the history of Christianity or Islam is known, then, of course, the resemblances were put down to the fact that these religions had been diffused, each from some one center. However remote the spot where Christians or Moslems were found, nobody, not even the wildest theorist, ventured to suggest that these religions had arisen independently there. If, however, the early history of any widespread feature, the belief in witchcraft, for example, was unknown, it was assumed as a matter of course that it could not have been diffused from one center, but must have originated independently wherever it was found, in response to some stimulus acting upon a tendency supposed to be innate in the human mind.

It was the same with material inventions. It was known that the Africans had acquired their guns from foreigners, and the fact that these guns supplied a felt want was therefore not regarded as showing that local demand had led to local supply. But the Africans also had bows and arrows. These also supplied a felt want, and judging by the history of guns it might have been thought at least possible that local demand had been met by foreign supply. It was, however, not so thought. The history of bows and arrows was unknown, and it was therefore assumed, as a matter of course, that they had been independently invented by every African tribe which possessed them. It was, in fact, regarded as axiomatic that if you do not know where anything came from, you are entitled to assume that it originated wherever you happen to find it.

Professor R. B. Dixon (*The Building of Cultures,* p. 223) attempted to give scientific backing to this very unscientific view. "That diffusion," he says,

> *is responsible for a large number of apparently disconnected similar traits is probable, but there remains a considerable residuum for which independent origin is the only rational explanation. For common sense and the laws of probability must be applied to all cases, and when an explanation by diffusion requires us to assume that the extremely improbable or almost impossible has occurred, the* onus probandi *becomes very heavy. Where the physical difficulties in the way are very serious, we must refuse to be carried away by vague generalities and demand very concrete proof, and until such proof is forthcoming the alternative of independent invention or convergence must be preferred.* [Raglan's emphasis.] *That diffusion has been responsible for cultural development to a far greater extent than independent invention is quite certain, but occasional independent invention cannot, in the face of the evidence, be denied.*

In spite of the admission in the last sentence, what Professor Dixon would have us believe is that if in any part of the world we find people using a particular implement, we are bound to assume that they invented that implement unless it is otherwise proved. To do this he has to resort to a good deal of special pleading. In the first place what is "extremely improbable" is not, as he suggests, a matter of fact, but merely a speculation, quite valueless as a proof. Then he tells us that if we do not know which of two alternative hypotheses is true, one of the two becomes "the only rational explanation" and is to be accepted without any proof at all; the other would require "very concrete proof." In any doubtful case diffusion must be rejected, although it has affected culture "to a far greater extent" than independent invention.

Professor Dixon also urges us to apply "common sense and the laws of probability," but there are no relevant laws of probability, and common sense is quite inapplicable. Common sense is the result of experience gained in our daily life, and can no more help us to decide questions of human origins than it can entitle us to express an opinion on the theory of relativity. The common-sense view is, and must remain, that the sun goes round the earth. We reject that view because we have, in that particular case, passed from the realm of common sense into that of scientific induction. . . .

Such a travesty of logic could never have found acceptance were it not that it supplies a felt want, the want of many scientists and nearly all scholars for a theory which will help them to put a ring-fence round the subject of their studies. If classical scholars had to admit that Greek culture, far from being the product of the special genius of the Greek race, imposed upon the general genius of the human race, was really the fruit of a tree whose roots extended as far afield as Egypt, Mesopotamia, Persia, and even India, they would have either to widen the range of their studies or abandon their pretense to a localized omniscience. And if Americanists had to admit the possibility, which becomes more and more a probability, that the civilization of Middle America came from Asia, then they would be reduced to the status of experts in a group of provincial cultures.

One of the greatest dangers to our civilization is that nearly all knowledge is in the minds of professionals, of people who are paid to teach or act upon a certain set of supposed facts, and who take as an insult or a threat any suggestion that these supposed facts are inaccurate or incomplete. To all of these (and to all nationalists) the theory of diffusion is anathema, since it lets the deep sea into scores of little ponds, upon which little experts sail fleets of toy boats. These toy boats cannot survive in the sea of diffusion, which requires a well-found vessel carrying a large crew.

Yet the hypothesis of diffusion merely assumes that prehistoric times were not very different from historic times. Among the chief features of recorded history are conquests, migrations, and colonizations which completely transformed the cultures of vast areas. In modern times we have the European colonization of America, Australia, and South Africa. Earlier we have the Roman conquest of Western Europe and the Arab conquest of North Africa. All these movements have, so far as the great majority of the inhabitants are concerned, submerged the previous cultures. Even where the earlier inhabitants have not been absorbed, as in South Africa, they are rapidly adopting the culture of their conquerors. North Africa has been the home of great civilizations, Egyptian, Carthaginian, Greek, and Roman, yet there is little in its present culture which antedates the Arab conquest. We see Buddhism spreading from India to China and Japan; Islam from Arabia to Nigeria, Central Asia, and Java; not to speak of the spread of Christianity. Similarly we see such inventions as gunpowder, printing, steam power, and electricity spreading all over the world and displacing older devices.

The hypothesis of multiple invention assumes that though such movements have been going on ever since the beginnings of recorded history, nothing of the sort ever happened where there was no recorded history. It encourages us to suppose that diffusion to Britain began with Julius Caesar; to America with Columbus, and to Central Africa with Livingstone.

The hypothesis of diffusion, on the contrary, is that history merely records some of the more recent incidents in a process which has been going on for untold millennia, probably since the time, some half-million years ago, when man first appeared. Diffusion depends, of course, on transport and communication, and these have recently been speeded up, but it is often forgotten that all the great movements of peoples and cultures which took place before 1840 depended on the use of sails and of wheeled vehicles, means of transport which have been in use for at least five thousand years, or two thousand years before the beginning of European history. That culture movements covering vast areas did in fact take place in prehistoric times is clear from the researches of archaeologists, who are largely engaged in tracing types of pots, bronze axes, and other artefacts across the length of continents. It is no exaggeration to say that every excavation of any importance affords evidence of previously unsuspected cultural relationships between more or less remote areas. Except where there was some form of script our knowledge of these relationships is confined to material objects, but observation of what is happening today shows that there is never any considerable transmission of material culture without a corresponding transmission of ideas and beliefs. It is possible, of course, to transmit objects of iron or glass by mere barter without any exchange of ideas at all, but impossible to acquire the arts of iron-working or glass-blowing without a good deal of social intercourse. No serious student believes that these arts were invented more than once, and the same applies, as we shall see later, to many other arts. It is absurd to suppose that people traveled about Europe, Asia, and Africa teaching people by signs to work iron, and then returned to their homeland leaving no other trace of their presence, yet this is another of the absurdities implicit in the case for independent invention. It is obviously possible, one would think, that the people who transmitted the art of iron-working might at the same time transmit stories or superstitions connected therewith, yet there are writers galore who will assure us that such stories and superstitions, however similar, are never transmitted, but are the product of the local "folk" wherever they are found.

We shall later discuss the "folk" as inventors; what we must here note is that the fact of independent invention has never been established. That is to say, that no invention, discovery, custom, belief, or even story is known for certain to have originated in two separate cultures. . . .

The problems of diffusion, then, are not concerned with whether it has taken place. It has taken place from the earliest times, and is at the present moment going on all round us. The real problems are how anything comes to be invented at all, and how, having been invented at some one place, it finds its way about the world. . . .

*   *   *

We know that our own civilization, in all but its latest phases, was not evolved locally, but derived from the Mediterranean. We know that Greece derived its civilization from Asia Minor, Crete, and Egypt. We, like the Greeks and Romans, have improved upon the civilization which we received from outside, but it is quite untrue to say that we evolved our own civilization. It is then clearly not the fact that civilization has *everywhere* been evolved out of savagery, and to say that it has *anywhere* been evolved out of savagery is a guess which cannot be supported by any evidence. As Niebuhr[1] . . . remarked, "no single example can be brought forward of an actually savage people having independently become civilized." So far as we *know,* all civilization has been evolved from preexisting civilization, not from savagery.

Of the real beginnings of culture we know nothing for certain, and it is very doubtful whether we ever shall. It seems likely that the cradle-land of the human race was in Southwestern Asia, where was also the seat of the earliest civilizations, yet there are fewer traces of "primitive man" there than in many other parts of the world. Whether this is because the earliest cultures are beneath the silt of the Euphrates or the Indus, or whether their remains still await the chance disturbance of the surface at some hitherto unsuspected spot we cannot say. . . .

[1] Reference is to Barthold Georg Niebuhr (1776–1831), noted German historian and statesman, who is best known for his innovative work in Roman History.—Ed.

Against this it might be urged that we cannot suppose man to have been created in an already civilized condition, and therefore the earlier steps on the road to civilization must have been taken by savages, that is to say, by people exactly like modern savages. And if that is so, then modern savages, if left to themselves, must be capable of initiating civilizations. But the beginning of this contention should be to show that modern savages, when left alone, do make progress, and, as I have tried to show, all the evidence points in the opposite direction.

And it is not only modern evidence that we have. We know that man has been on earth for something like half a million years, yet up till about ten thousand years ago the highest men had got no farther than the condition in which the lowest savages now exist. As Elliot Smith points out, . . . it cannot therefore be maintained that man has an instinctive tendency to civilize himself. . . .

. . . There is no doubt that savages are capable of being civilized; the point is that they are incapable of civilizing themselves. It is clear from the facts outlined above that not only must the theory that the Stone Age savages of Europe civilized themselves through their own instinct of progress go, but with it must go the theory from which it is really inseparable, that of "stages of progress." The domestication of animals and the development of agriculture will be discussed later, but here we must note the belief, quite recently extinct among scientists, that the domestication of animals was an "easier" process than agriculture, and that all over the world man progressed naturally from hunting to pastoralism, and thence to agriculture. We have just seen that in Northern and Western Europe neither pastoralism nor agriculture was a local development, but that both were introduced from the southeast at or about the same time. It is now realized that many pastoralists, such as the nomad Arabs, Tatars, and Somalis, are at a higher level of culture than many savage cultivators, and that many cultivators, for example, the Mayas and the Polynesians, have been quite ignorant of pastoralism. Whatever the early history of all these peoples, it is clear that the theory that agriculture is something that people naturally add to pastoralism on their way up the cultural scale cannot be sustained. There is, on the contrary, reason to believe that agriculture came before and not after the domestication of animals, at least of all animals except the dog.

We shall see later that not only cereal agriculture and the domestication of animals, but many other inventions and discoveries, can be traced, either with certainty or great probability, to one part of the world, a region which centers in Persia, and extends to Egypt, North India, and China. These origins can be traced not merely by means of such artefacts as are dug up, but by the distribution of traits at the dawn of history, as indicated by inscriptions, drawings, and carvings. We may suppose that man was evolved from the ape within this region, and carried thence many simple traits in his wanderings towards the Cape of Good Hope or Cape Horn, but all the discoveries and inventions upon which European civilization, that is to say, Graeco-Roman civilization, was based, seem to have been made within this region at a time, about the fourth millennium B.C., when the rest of the world was inhabited, so far as it was inhabited at all, by savages who, in the only area in which we know anything of them, were definitely on the down-grade.

The question then arises, were the people of Persia, Mesopotamia, etc., when they began to make all these discoveries and invent all these traits, savages? The answer must be that if they were they must have been very different from any savages, either ancient or modern, of whom we know anything, since these latter, as we must repeat, are not known ever to have invented or discovered anything. "Man," as Dr. Harrison says, . . . "did very well before he was a man at all, and no one has given any reason why he ceased to be an ape." It is generally agreed that the ancestors of *Homo sapiens,* at any rate, emerged at one time and in one place, and we can only suppose that their emergence was due to some special and localized stimulus. That was sufficient to turn apes into what we may call palaeolithic men. It is possible that another special and localized stimulus was required to set man on the road to civilization. . . .

*   *   *

We have seen that many of the principal discoveries and inventions upon which our civilization is based can be traced with considerable probability to an area with its focus near the head of the Persian Gulf, and such evidence as there is suggests that they were made by ingenious priests as a means of facilitating the performance of religious ritual. It is at least possible that animals were first domesticated for convenience in sacrifice and that the first use of the plow was as a method of symbolically fertilizing the soil; the first wheel may have been a labor-saving device for keeping the sun on its course, and metal-working may have started with the making of imitation suns in gold; the first bow and arrow may have ensured victory by symbolically destroying enemies at a distance; mummification kept the dead king ritually alive, and the kite conveyed his spirit to the sky. There is *some* evidence to support all these suggestions, and its cumulative effect strengthens the theory as a whole, the theory, that is, that civilization originated in ritual, though of course a great deal more evidence would be required to establish it. Alternative theories have no evidence to support them at all. . . .

. . . We have, in fact, good reason to believe that among the Ancient Babylonians and Egyptians, as to a great extent among the modern Hindus, ritual was regarded as the prime motive power in the world. It was only by means of ritual that the sun was induced to rise and the rain to fall; that birth was caused, disease cured and death averted; in short, it was believed that ritual is productive of all good, and destructive of all evil. This belief, in various forms, is still found all over the world. There is, however, no reason to believe that it is in any way natural or instinctive; the probability is, that like all forms of culture, it was diffused from some one area, probably in Southwestern Asia. For belief in ritual, whether we call it magical or religious, depends on belief in the priest, the man who knows and performs the ritual, and it can hardly be doubted that the priest is a product of culture. And he may well have been the father of civilization. For in communities dominated by ritual, as we have reason to believe that the communities in which civilization originated were, the priest was the repository of all knowledge. There must, of course, have been knowledge other than of ritual, but all knowledge was dependent on ritual. The priestly colleges were centers of wealth and leisure, the only ones that there were, and therefore the only places in which experiments could be performed. But since ritual was the main interest of the priests, their experiments would be based upon the requirements of ritual, which, as it developed, would stimulate fresh experiments. . . .

As long as ritual is expanding and developing, so long can the inventor find shelter under its wing; but ritual expansion has seldom occurred. We have reason to believe that the vast ritual complex associated with the divine kingship was developed in the Ancient East, in the same regions as, and most probably in association with, the various inventions and discoveries connected with the growing of corn, the domestication of sheep and cattle, pottery and the use of metals, which we have discussed in previous chapters.

From the Ancient East the stream flowed east and west. . . .

Rushton Coulborn
THE SEVEN CENTERS OF CIVILIZATION

Contrasting the arguments of the hyperdiffusionists—who maintain that the origin of civilization occurred once and only once—other scholars have argued that the rise of civilization was not an isolated phenomenon, but had multiple beginnings, in different parts of the world at different times. This view has been set forth by the English-born and -educated historian Rushton Coulborn in The Origin of Civilized Societies, *which he wrote to illustrate that there have been seven primary civilizations and that the origin of none of these can be attributed to diffusion. In addition to his academic experience in England, Coulborn served from 1939–1965 as chairman of the Department of History of Atlanta University. Professor Coulborn died in 1968.*

Civilized societies have been in existence for about six or six and a half millennia. It cannot be doubted that they are the greatest social achievement humanity has yet made. According to the criteria of differences used in this study, there have been fourteen distinct civilized societies, or a few more if certain minor formations are counted. Of the fourteen, four exist today fully recognizable, and remnants of a few others in recognizable, or unrecognizable, shapes.

The term "civilized" is reserved here for the large societies to be identified forthwith, and the term "civilization" for their high culture considered abstractly.

The earliest civilized societies were the Egyptians and Mesopotamian societies, which arose in the valleys respectively of the Nile and of the Tigris and Euphrates, probably in the fifth millennium B.C. It

Selections from Rushton Coulborn, *The Origin of Civilized Societies* (copyright © 1959 by Princeton University Press; Princeton Paperback, 1969), pp. 3–30. Omission of footnotes. Reprinted by permission of Princeton University Press.

is not possible to decide whether one was earlier than the other; nor, for most purposes, would it be particularly useful to do so. The Indian Society arose first in the valley of the Indus where that river passes through Sind and the Punjab and possibly also in the valley of a now dry sister river of the Indus, usually called the Great Mihran by those who think it existed. Whether the Indian Society originated earlier, later, or about the same time as the Egyptian and Mesopotamian societies is not known, but possibly a few centuries later.

The Cretan Society arose in the island of Crete and subsequently extended into the Cyclades, the Peloponnese, and perhaps elsewhere. It originated about 3000 B.C. or somewhat earlier. The Chinese Society arose in the Yellow River Valley and on the river's tributaries in north China where the river passes between Shensi and Shansi and through Honan. Its time of origin is not clear, but is most likely to have been in the first half of the third millennium B.C.

In the New World two other societies arose. The Middle American Society arose somewhere within a broad territory beginning in the north with the Mexican states of Vera Cruz, Guanajuato, and Michoacan, and covering the rest of Mexico southward and eastward, British Honduras, Guatemala, Honduras, and some of El Salvador. It is becoming clear that the society was much scattered within this territory from an early time in its existence.

The Andean Society arose in all likelihood on three or more rivers which cross the northern part of the Peruvian coastal desert, the rivers Chicama, Moche, and Virú and perhaps others. Eventually the society extended to the valleys of some thirty-five odd rivers which cross the desert farther south, and also moved up and well over the Andes. These two societies originated during the second millennium B.C., the Middle American Society towards the beginning of the second millennium, and the Andean Society towards the end of it.

Following [Arnold] Toynbee and Alfred Weber, I call these seven societies the primary civilized societies since they were, each within its general region, the earliest civilized societies. This book is a study of how the seven primary civilized societies arose; it is a study, that is to say, of how civilization began. The societies arose in very special circumstances, of which the chief was change of climate in certain regions at the end of the last Pleistocene Ice Age. The regions are today desert or steppe, and it was their conversion to that dry condition which drove some of their human inhabitants to make a long series of cultural and social changes, to migrate in various directions and on a number of occasions, and eventually to form civilized societies. . . .

Every primary civilized society was formed by the amalgamation, in a special kind of environment, of a large number of primitive societies; the term "conglomeration" will be applied here to the formative process. There have been many kinds of primitive societies in the human career. Anthropologists are accustomed to use such terms as "folk" or "nonliterate" to denote all of them together, but there will be little occasion in this study for those usages. The primitive societies involved in the origin of civilized societies were among the most advanced societies of their times. They were of tens, hundreds, perhaps sometimes of thousands of persons, organized, at least when settled, on some kind of kinship basis. They were able to live in sedentary villages fixed as to place for a period of years, but all those involved in the origin of civilized societies were, or had recently been, migrants from other places to the sites in which the civilized societies arose. All, or almost all, of them had grain agriculture.

All of them were very largely dependent upon grain agriculture for their subsistence, but the grains they raised varied from region to region, chiefly wheat and barley in the westerly region of the Old World and in India, one or more millets and kaoliang, possibly barley, even possibly rice, in China, maize in the New World. They all raised other vegetables also, but their dependence on these varied widely from case to case. In fact, except for the large dependence on grain raising, all their common activities varied much from group to group. Thus, none of them could maintain their villages—those they occupied before migration to the sites of the future civilized societies—in the same place indefinitely, for after some years they would have exhausted the soil by repeated cropping. How soon a village had to move must have varied greatly, however, chiefly with the quality of the soil, but also to some extent with varying methods of cultivation. Most villages increased rather rapidly in population, but the rate of increase probably varied a good deal as between different regions. Parts of the increased population could and certainly did hive off from time to time, but the consequent increase in a whole district required general expansion, and must have led to longer and longer and more and more dangerous migrations. Probably some villagers had to move as often as every three years, the majority at all sorts of intervals up to a generation and more.

All the villagers had pottery, but it varied a great deal in quality; in most cases it was good. They all made cloth by spinning and weaving, or by variations of those practices. Certainly, they did not all have domesticated animals: in the New World such animals were very few, or entirely lacking; in the Old World, they varied from region to region, but were numerous in the westerly region. All the villagers hunted, and continued to hunt after the civilized societies emerged, but their reliance upon game for food must have varied a good deal. Their modes of housing themselves varied, but that perhaps does not matter very much for present purposes.

All the primitive societies had beliefs about the physical world in which they lived, beliefs which required the existence of controlling powers, not easily discernible to man, but actively interested in man's doings, and prepared to interfere if man did things they did not like. Undoubtedly, all the societies were much concerned with the attitude of the controlling powers toward the growth of the plants cultivated.

It is not known for certain that grain agriculture was a necessary basis for the formation of a civilized society, but it looks, on the evidence, as if this were so. On the Andean coastal plain, near the mouths of the rivers in whose valleys the civilized society subsequently arose—but very probably not in the valleys themselves—a series of very simple societies, having agriculture but not grain agriculture, established themselves about 2500 B.C. They probably made some sort of use of the rivers, but they continued to live in their simple way for a thousand years without change and without producing any sign—visible to archaeologists—of the beginnings of civilized life. The environment for civilization was at hand, but the peoples had not the cultural basis on which to begin to create a civilization: this is how the situation appears, but the assumption that it was so remains an informed assumption, nothing more. Guesses that there were "marsh Arabs" in southern Mesopotamia, or "fen-dwellers" on the lower Yellow River in China, before the grain cultivators came and settled there are quite insubstantial. Mesolithics and palaeolithics lived indeed in the Kom Ombo Plain, contiguous to the Upper Nile in Nubia, for millennia, and palaeolithics lived near the Indus at Rohri and Sukkur in northern Sind. It seems reasonable to think that palaeolithics and mesolithics, and (if any) fen-dwellers and marsh Arabs, lacked the cultural basis from which to begin the creation of a civilized society, however alluring or compulsive the environment in which they found themselves.

It deserves mention, even though it is abundantly obvious, that a culture having grain agriculture together with an assortment of other useful practices did not of itself by some inherent determinism move on to civilization. Vast numbers of primitive societies with such cultures survived for thousands of years with little change; some survive even now. These things have to be borne in mind because the majority of current books on the subject still describe civilization as a bundle of culture traits, many of them throwing in agriculture without adequate distinction from the rest. In this book agriculture will be treated . . . separately as, to the best of our understanding, the key achievement of man preliminary to civilization, while civilization itself will not be considered as a sum of culture traits.

Another caution, but a less obvious one: civilized societies arose within very special physical environments, but that does not mean that every time grain-cultivating primitives arrived in such an environment a civilized society resulted. We have a relatively good knowledge of the early settlements in the Nile valley; perhaps our knowledge covers something about all of them. The first three types of settlers, all grain-raisers, showed no signs of creating a civilized society even though they lived in their new habitat for some centuries. Of course, they may have entered on a course toward civilization; there is, it may be supposed, more likelihood that they did so than that the earliest, non-grain-raising settlers on the Andean coast did so: the difficulty may merely be that there are no signs of it which an archaeologist can detect.

Again, there are grain-raisers and grain-raisers, and perhaps some grain-raisers could not rise to the initiation of civilization. If they could not, then perhaps their methods of cultivation were not good enough, or perhaps some other trait we have not perceived was needed as well as grain-cultivation. Or, yet again, perhaps there were crucial differences between the various sites, even perhaps between the various river valley sites, in which civilized societies arose, such that for some sites greater preliminary attainments on the part of the settlers were required than for other sites. Here we reach the sphere of the unknown.

Ignorance, then, is freely admitted. But certain suggestions may be made as a start toward dispelling it. One is that the primitives who left their old habitats and migrated to the special kinds of place in which civilized societies arose probably did so because they were in some danger; their survival may have been threatened, and they may have migrated in a state of great agitation. I think it may be taken for granted at least that there were strong reasons for the migrations and that the reasons were not in themselves pleasant; the migrants were not, for example, people getting along fairly well in their old habitat who developed an optimistic conviction that life would be even better in some other place. As we have already seen, the migrations were undertaken at a time of desiccation so that the likelihood of threats to their survival is a large one.

A second suggestion is that the migration from the old habitat to the new is unlikely to have been easy. It is unlikely to have allayed fears, if any, with which the migrants set out. There may well have been casualties on the way; there almost certainly were on some of the migrations. Some whole groups of migrants have got lost in deserts and died en route, but this is only of significance for the origin of civilized societies if it was known to other groups who got through with some success to the new habitat; it may have been known to them.

A third suggestion is that on migration a social organization different from that of a settled society, even of a settled society which expects to migrate from time to time, is needed. This may have been of little consequence in the case of very short migrations—and some of the migrations were short—but it can have been of large consequence in cases where they were not short. The old bonds of primitive societies may have weakened somewhat, and possibly there were leaders on the migrations who acquired more authority than the elders of a more or less sedentary clan or tribe.

A fourth suggestion is that the new habitats were in no case easy to settle in; this follows from the assumption, already made, that simpler peoples could not make much of them and in known cases probably settled on the outer edge of the site and not right in it. This suggestion is one founded on a fair amount of evidence. The most important evidence is of adaptation to the conditions of water supply. . . . Here it need only be added that conditions in the new habitat, however much they varied from case to case, are unlikely to have eased the fears and anxieties we have supposed the migrants to have experienced before and during their migrations—even if the conditions may soon have become such as to set up hopes alongside the fears, or effectively to nourish hopes which already existed. Nor, if any special discipline was developed on migration, were conditions in the new habitat such as to encourage its loosening.

Finally, out of these various suggestions about fears, hopes, and discipline a thesis may be proposed to the effect that new religious developments probably arose in the minds of the migrants before they left their old homes, while they were migrating, and after their resettlement. It is possible to find support for this thesis in surviving myths and from archaeological sources. . . . Analogies, too, are powerful enforcements of the thesis, and these may be briefly outlined at once.

The most telling analogies, I think, are the religious movements which have occurred among primitives in recent times when their ways of life have been endangered, usually by encounter with the ways of civilized societies. Many of these happened in North America as the "Indians" there succumbed to Western colonization. Some others occurred very recently in Pacific islands during the 1941 war with invasion of armed forces of the belligerents. In these cases, charismatic leadership almost always arose, a leadership which was not often, if indeed ever, wholly reactionary, but instead sought to combine new practices with old. Although such new practices in these cases were mostly learned from the civilized intruders, they could presumably have been improvised out of untaught experience where there were no human opponents from whom to learn, as must have happened to the early settlers in the sites of the primary civilized societies; and those settlers who were not the earliest may well have learned some things from those who had preceded them. . . .

How does a civilized society differ from a primitive society? Certain easy answers may be given to this question though none of them, nor all of them together, are more than a part of the whole answer. . . .

The first easy answer is that a civilized society is very much larger than a primitive society, hundreds or thousands of times as large. It may be said too that it is more complex, but greater complexity is only a function of other differences, of which the difference in size is the main one. Some of the other differences are specifiable, and most of them turn out also to be merely quantitative: a civilized society gains more knowledge of the physical world than a primitive society does, and develops a larger apparatus of thought; it has more wealth in absolute terms, more per head of population usually, and so forth.

There are difficulties about most criteria which have customarily been used to distinguish civilized from primitive societies. It is not, for example, correct to say that all civilized societies have writing even if it is correct so say that no primitive societies have (unless they have borrowed it from a civilized society, and such borrowings do not count in the distinction): the Andean Society had no true system of writing, and there were regions in the Middle American Society where there was scarcely a true practice of writing either. Moreover, writing appeared at very different times in the historic development of different civilized societies: in Mesopotamia it was slowly evolved in a period of small states when administration was no large problem, whereas in Egypt and Crete it was adopted relatively quickly at the juncture when the respective societies were being politically unified. This difference reinforces the cases of the Andean and Middle American societies in showing that writing is not a necessity of civilized status, but simply an important device which may be used in a civilized society for various purposes.

If we seek to trace writing back to its origin, the search is likely to lead to mnemonic devices, to hunting-signs scratched on trees or stones, to marks on pots, to conventional designs made on objects marking places of assembly, and the like; and all of these are found in primitive societies. Almost certainly, it remains true to say that primitive societies do not have writing; what has happened in most, but not all, civilized societies is that one kind of thing, marks serving to convey simple information, has grown quantitatively until another kind of thing has emerged, and the quantitative change must be said to have turned into a qualitative change. This is the real significance of the occurrence of writing in most civilized societies and its nonoccurrence in primitive societies. And, certainly, there are other practices and institutions which differ in the same way as between civilized and primitive societies. Perhaps indeed something of the sort should be said of civilized societies considered as wholes by contrast with primitive societies—but it is early in the argument to accept that conclusion.

The distinction which finds towns or cities in a civilized society and not in a primitive society is on much the same footing as the one which uses writing—until, as sometimes happens, its authors claim too much for it. There probably were no towns in primitive societies before civilized societies came into existence, although that is not a proven fact; there may have been some rather large villages, at any rate in the pre-civilized Near East. From the Middle American Society doubt is thrown on the distinction from the opposite standpoint, for it is clear that in the Maya part of that society, which was the leading part of it, there was nothing which can properly be described as a town. But most civilized societies had towns and few, if any, primitive societies did. To go on from this to say that the substance of civilization resides in the fact that a society has towns is, however, claiming far too much for the distinction. It is a mistaking of result for cause, and indeed of only one kind of result among many. A number of the villages of the early stages of development of a civilized society were destined to grow into towns, and they usually began quite early to manifest an urban character. Hence they serve well for diagnosis of the emergence of civilization, but in fact the civilization was in all cases present before towns appeared.

There is one distinction between civilized and primitive societies which is perfectly clear and is not only quantitative: civilized societies are all subject to a cyclical movement of rise and fall in the course of their development, but no similar movement occurs in the development of primitive societies. Rhythms dependent on the seasons affect all primitive societies, of course, but the cyclical movements of civilized societies are of millennial span. Sorokin has done more than any other scholar to show the importance of these movements. He analyzes the cycle into three phases, distinguishing them in his own special terms.[1] The three phases will not require close study in this book, but they will be called, where it is required to mention them, "age of faith," "age of reason," and "age of fulfillment."

Two quantitative factors, both of them very great, are involved in this disparity of development between civilized and primitive societies. The two factors are a great difference in rate of change and a

---

[1] Coulborn refers here to Pitrim A. Sorokin's use of psychological-sociological terms —the "ideational" culture, the "idealistic" culture and the "sensate" culture—to designate the three phases in the development of Western civilization. Pitrim A. Sorokin, *Social and Cultural Dynamics* (New York, 1941), IV, 138–142; 428–432.—Ed.

great difference in power of control over the physical environment. Many primitive societies scarcely change at all in thousands of years, whereas civilized societies do not remain unchanged even for centuries. Primitive societies, in general, can remain unchanged so long as their environment does so, but if their environment itself changes, they must adapt themselves to the change, or migrate, or perish. It is exceptional for civilized man to retreat before changes in his environment, though he has done so; he usually succeeds in adapting his environment to himself. Nor has any civilized society perished yet, either through causes arising in its environment, or through any other cause; at worst, it has been transformed into a new civilized society.

There is, then, in civilized societies a quality, absent from primitive societies, which impels both rapidity of development and domination over the physical environment and shows itself obscurely in the cyclical rise and fall movement.

We turn now to a different matter, an analytical examination of civilization.

In his Huxley Memorial Lecture (for 1945), Kroeber distinguishes between the style, or form, of a civilization, its cultural content, and the values it attains from time to time.[2] We shall not be much concerned in this study with values, for, even if these are inherent in a civilization from its origin, they are little developed at that time. With style and content, however, we are essentially concerned.

The style of a civilization is perceived as its aesthetic aspect; it is exhibited in everything the society produces and does, preeminently in its arts, but also in its thought, its politics, its institutions, its traditions, and in all its ways. It is possible to qualify a society's style, to comment upon it, to judge it even, yet hardly to describe it. It is the "Chineseness" of what is Chinese, the "Egyptianness" of what is Egyptian, the "Westernness" of what is Western. It changes with time and with place and yet remains always recognizable as the product of the same society. Those who get to know the style of any civilized society recognize it wherever they see it, for it is the mark of individuality of the society. Thus the fourteen civilized societies . . . are distinguished from one another by their special styles.

---

[2] Reference is to A. L. Kroeber, an American anthropologist noted for his seminal contributions to physical anthropology, archaeology, and ethnology.—Ed.

This is the criterion of individuation employed in this book, and all opinions and arguments which ignore, minimize, or deny this manner of individuation are rejected as wrong.

The cultural content of a civilization is what the anthropologist ordinarily calls culture traits or complexes, such practical traits as plowing, weaving, and pottery, such theoretical ones as divination, magic, and art themes, and probably many abstract and abstruse things which can be discerned by scholars only with difficulty. Culture traits and complexes can be diffused from one society to another, between civilized and primitive societies as well as between different societies of the same kind. Diffusion of traits between civilized societies has sometimes been taken to mean that the societies sharing a number of traits are parts of the same society, but this is only true when the style of expression of the traits is also the same in each case. In itself, the occurrence of the same, or similar, traits in more than one place has no bearing upon whether the same society exists in the two or more places in question. Each society inventing a culture trait, or receiving it in diffusion from another society, stamps the sign of its own style upon the product of the trait so that the products of different societies look different, unless perhaps for a very short time after a society has newly acquired the trait.

Diffusion can carry large complexes or small traits from one society to another. According to Kroeber, it can carry a mere "stimulus" from one society to another, that is to say, a generic idea without any particulars of a trait attached. Diffusion can spread far by its two methods, migration of peoples and communication of ideas and practices. It can even be worldwide, given a long enough time, though it rarely was worldwide in the late prehistoric times with which this book is concerned. Often it is difficult to know whether the appearance of a certain trait in a certain society was due to diffusion or to separate invention, but, where there is doubt, I incline toward diffusion, especially in the case of any intricate complex or association of traits. Diffusion was never a cause or means of origin of a civilized society, but only a vehicle of its spread; that, however, is a rather special matter which will be further discussed below.

The enquiry so far, then, suggests that we learn little about a society from the presence in its culture of particular traits. Most traits do not even show whether the society is civilized or primitive. Writing and towns create a presumption of civilization, but do not afford proof. As a rule, a particular trait or complex conveys, by itself, no information about a society which has it except its own existence in the culture. If a society is found to develop rapidly and to move historically through cycles of rise and fall, then the society is civilized. Any society, civilized or primitive, is to be identified by its style.

It must be supposed that at the foundation of the seven primary civilized societies the earliest cultural content was that brought by the immigrating settlers into the sites. It stands to reason, however, that the founders very soon invented a host of special practices, necessary to the novel kind of life they were developing in the sites they had found for themselves, and that these practices took a large place in the culture. Traits and complexes diffused from other civilized societies, and from primitive societies as well, were received from time to time, but there is no evidence whatever that any of the seven societies began as a mere colony, complete with culture content, style, and inherent or potential values, sent out by another civilized society. On the contrary, there is clear evidence that each society got started independently, for each one produced its own distinctive style, different from that of every other one, recognizably different even to a very moderately discerning eye. The independent start is confirmed for four out of the seven primary civilized societies by archaeological evidence of the immigration and settlement of peoples in the sites. Nor is inference of analogous immigration and settlement hard to support for the other three societies; it is almost certain.

There are certain false doctrines current about these fundamental matters. The doctrines destroy themselves when carried to their logical conclusions, and it is necessary now to bring the doctrines forward and let them show their quality.

One false doctrine is that of Sir Mortimer Wheeler which purports to find the origin of the Indian Society in Mesopotamia. It appears on first acquaintance an interesting doctrine, for Wheeler proposes that "ideas have wings" and that "the *idea* of civilization came to the land of the Indus from the land of the Twin Rivers." On examination, the *idea* decomposes into a series of different ideas, the idea of writing, of sealing, and others—only the bare idea being shared in each case by the two societies and all the details of application being different. We need not quarrel with this argument purely as an argument to establish a theory, for it is simply Kroeber's stimulus diffusion.

But Wheeler's application of the theory is quite wrong. His "idea of civilization," actually a very complex structure of purely abstract ideas all of them interrelated—and, as such, rather difficult to credit —he supposes to have been brought from Mesopotamia and planted in India precisely as from a mother country to a colony. Such things have happened not infrequently in history, but when they have the colony has received from the mother country not only ideas and culture traits but also, and of crucial significance, the style of the mother country. Since Indian style is quite different from Mesopotamian, the notion falls to the ground. It fails to account for the actual origin of the Indian Society; appropriately, but of course fundamentally, modified, it may well account for culture traits and ideas which came to India *after* the origin of the civilized society there.

Another false doctrine having a certain interest is Gordon Childe's supposedly materialistic doctrine. This doctrine allows the separate origin of the three valley societies—the Egyptian, Mesopotamian, and Indian—but then proposes that in those societies, under the government of kings or priests, surplus wealth was saved up out of the food produced by the peasants to become capital for all the economic purposes of a civilized society, one of the purposes being trade with other societies for the raw materials which were in all cases lacking in the valleys. The other societies, at first primitive, thus acquired an initial fund of capital for themselves and so were able to convert themselves into urban (civilized) societies. But "this," says Childe, "is not a case of like producing like"; as a matter of fact, Crete and other later societies differed more from "their reputed ancestors" than the ancestors differed among themselves. Moreover, the borrowing of capital by the later from the earlier societies "is most obvious in the case of cultural capital. Even today we use the Egyptians' calendar and the [Mesopotamian] Sumerians' divisions of the day and the hour."

Cultural capital retains, verbally, a Marxist sound, but in fact calendars and the like are culture traits within the ordinary anthropological meaning of the term, while to say that the passage of cultural capital from an old to a new society "is not a case of like producing like" is rather a bland admission that borrowing of culture traits is not all that happens when a new society is formed—an admission, but no explanation. In fact, great as Childe's services have been to prehistory, this doctrine is not among them: it says nothing we do not already know and omits more of that than it includes. Moreover, the doctrine is not really in the hard currency of materialism: when cultural capital displaces financial capital, Marx is stood upon his head and Hegel hath his revenge!

Childe's doctrine does show, nevertheless, too great a deference to material things, for it is ultimately a doctrine which requires of necessity a certain physiography, invariable in its major features, for the origin of civilized societies, namely the physiography of great river valleys. In this book a strong probability will be set up that the physiographic factor was much more variable than this and, as a corollary, that the participation of the human mind in the creation of the primary civilized societies was the greater.

It is to be noticed that both Childe and Wheeler witness unwittingly to the soundness of Kroeber's discernment that cultural content is not all that is involved in the phenomenon of civilization. Childe does so when he admits that like does not produce like and Wheeler when he seeks to strip civilization down to an idea. Both obscurely perceive vital differences, but cannot conceive them as differences of style.

Robert Heine-Geldern appears—but for a single cautionary footnote—to think that civilization is in fact culture traits and that all civilization is one, having originated in the Near East of the Old World; the latter he certainly does think, whatever he means by protesting that he does not intend to propound so simple a theory as that of Elliot Smith and W. J. Perry.[3] Heine-Geldern has done some valuable work in showing diffusion from the Near East to China and, some of it with Gordon Ekholm, from the Old World to the New,[4] but, in my opinion, he has shown nothing whatever about the origin of any of the primary civilized societies; on the contrary, he has brought into that problem only confusion.

[3] W. J. Perry was the most prolific disciple of G. Elliot Smith. For more information on Perry, see the selection by Glyn Daniel, "Diffusion and Distraction," reprinted below.—Ed.

[4] Reference here is to Gordon Ekholm's collaboration with Heine-Geldern in the research and publication of "Significant Parallels in the Symbolic Arts of Southern Asia and Middle America," *The Civilizations of Ancient America: Selected Papers of the XXIXth International Congress of Americanists,* ed. Sol Tax (Chicago, 1951), pp. 299–309.—Ed.

It is, in fact, not necessary here to pursue Heine-Geldern very far. Unlike Wheeler and Childe, he is not aware of differences of style, or he thinks them mere differences of detail not important enough to need explanation. His theory is an extremely simple one in terms of diffusion of culture traits alone. . . .

Diffusion had nothing to do with the origin of the primary civilized societies, or of any civilized societies. The diffusion which brought particular culture traits to the primary civilized societies could have had nothing to do with their origin, for it occurred after their origin. The diffusion which was important to the primary civilized societies is the diffusion which occurred before their origin, spreading many mesolithic practices throughout the world and a number of early agricultural practices over large regions. In that diffusion the cultural virtuosity of the Near East of the Old World was of capital importance, but it had no direct bearing upon the origin of civilized societies in the manner supposed by Heine-Geldern.

Glyn Daniel
DIFFUSION AND DISTRACTION

Glyn Daniel, an English scholar who has made a thorough study of the history of archaeology and who is a recognized authority on megalithic monuments, provides us with a judicious statement on the general spectrum of "hyperdiffusionist" thought. He is particularly critical of what he considers to be a rather simplistic treatment of some very complex problems on the part of the diffusionists. Daniel is the director of studies in archaeology and anthropology at St. John's College, Cambridge, and lecturer in archaeology in the University. He is the editor of the quarterly journal Antiquity, *and was the George Grant MacGurdy Lecturer in Prehistory at Harvard in 1971.*

We are, at first, mainly concerned with a very great man who was a Fellow of my own College in Cambridge, and who has been described by Warren Dawson, who edited a book of essays that form the biographical record of his life, as "one of the foremost anatomists and thinkers of his age," and also as "one of the outstanding intellectual

From Glyn Daniel: *The Idea of Prehistory* (London: C. A. Watts, 1962). Reprinted by permission of the publishers. Footnotes omitted.

personalities of his age." This man, Grafton Elliot Smith, was, and is, the outstanding example of one who fell, as those interested in prehistory are prone to fall, into that extraordinary and interesting intellectual error—the simplistic heresy of hyperdiffusion. . . . When I say this I must immediately explain how I am using this somewhat tendentious word. There were, in the second half of the nineteenth century . . . two explanations current as to the origin of the cultural changes which were manifest in the archaeological record, in history and in the modern world, and these explanations were usually centered over such things as the appearance, in two different parts of the world in the archaeological and ethnographical record, of apparently the same cultural features. One explanation was that these features had evolved separately and developed independently. The other was that a feature had spread from one area to another, that it had in fact been diffused—by trade, by the movement of people, or by culture contact. It is these two explanations of culture change that we refer to when we talk of evolution versus diffusion in the study of human cultural development. . . .

The controversy about all this begins when we start to argue about the relative importance of the factors in cultural change, and when we find people maneuvering themselves into, or pledging, positions in which only one explanation is possible. Adolf Bastian, the German scholar born in Bremen in 1826, is the out-and-out evolutionist who would not believe in diffusion, and a textbook example of such a person. He argued that by a general law the psychical unity of man everywhere produced similar ideas; different geographical environments might produce different responses, and there could of course be contacts in later historic times, but the basic idea was the psychic unity of man and, therefore, the independent evolution of culture. These ideas of Bastian's were a form of super-organic or cultural or social evolution. Others interested in anthropology flew to the opposite extreme and one such early diffusionist was [A. W.] Buckland¹ who, from 1878 onwards, set out in a series of papers— they have names like Primitive Agriculture, Prehistoric Intercourse between East and West, Four as a Sacred Number, etc.—a most violent and uncompromising hyperdiffusionism. According to Miss Buckland—and this is the key doctrine that is implicit in Elliot Smith

¹ From 1878–1900 Ms. Buckland presented a number of papers in defense of a radical diffusionist doctrine.—Ed.

and his followers—civilization was never, *never* independently acquired. It *could* not be and it *was* not. If you read Miss Buckland it will give you a foretaste of Elliot Smith, for she was writing about sun and serpent worship, and the spread of agriculture, weaving, pottery, and metals all over the earth.

Miss Buckland was writing her polemics as Grafton Elliot Smith was growing up in New South Wales and qualifying as a doctor at Sydney. It soon became clear to his chief at Sydney, Professor J. T. Wilson, that Elliot Smith was "meant for a life-work of scientific investigation rather than for the professional life of a medical practitioner." He was sent to England, became a Research Student at St. John's College, Cambridge, in 1896, and a Research Fellow there three years later. In 1900 Alexander Macalister, the Professor of Anatomy in Cambridge, conveyed to the young Elliot Smith an invitation to become the first occupant of the chair of anatomy at the Government Medical School at Cairo. The prime factor in the development of Elliot Smith's hyperdiffusionism was his stay in Egypt, . . . [and] mummification was the key-point in Elliot Smith's great Egyptocentric hyperdiffusionist doctrine. He believed that the technique of embalming was so complicated in Egypt that it could not have been invented identically, in all its complexity, anywhere else. Whenever, therefore, he came across the practice of embalming and mummification elsewhere he felt himself forced to conclude that it had spread from Egypt. "Little did I realize," he wrote in the preface to the second (1923) edition of his *Ancient Egyptians,* "when I was writing what was intended to be nothing more than a brief interim report . . . that this little book was destined to open up a new view —or rather to revise and extend an old and neglected method of interpretation of the history of civilization." Eagerly, he took up the diffusionist view with energy and zeal and with much of the ardor of a missionary.

. . . He had many enthusiastic disciples: as for example Wilfred Jackson who in 1917 wrote *Shells as Evidence of the Migrations of Early Culture* and Warren Dawson who wrote *Custom of Couvade* in 1929, but most of all his disciple was W. J. Perry who was first Reader in Comparative Religion in the University of Manchester when Elliot Smith was there, and then Reader of Cultural Anthropology in London when Elliot Smith moved there.

Perry was in many ways more enthusiastic and intransigent than his master. He wrote *The Children of the Sun* (1923), *The Origin of Magic and Religion* (1923), *The Megalithic Culture of Indonesia* (1918), and a general summary designed for the ordinary reader called *The Growth of Civilization.* This last book was first published in 1924 and was reissued in 1937 by Penguin Books Ltd. with all the widespread public appeal and wide circulation that such publication acquires. In the brief description on the jacket of the Penguin Books edition, it was said of Perry: "He is one of the chief supporters of the 'diffusionist' theory of the growth of culture." In an analysis of the growth of this theory he stresses that two things most affected Elliot Smith: the first, which we have mentioned, was embalming and mummification. The second was megalithic monuments; Elliot Smith had conceived the idea that the pyramids and mastabas of ancient Egypt were the prototypes of the megalithic monuments that are found, in a very wide diversity of form, all over the ancient world. Elliot Smith could not believe that mummification and megalithic architecture could have been invented more than once and he, therefore, concluded that both "practices" had been diffused from ancient Egypt.

He then began to see most of the elements of all culture as originating in Egypt, and defined a culture-complex of about thirty centuries ago which spread "like an exotic leaven"—the words are those of Elliot Smith and Perry—over the world taking with it civilization. This original Egyptian civilization was the Heliolithic or Archaic Civilization; Elliot Smith and Perry saw small groups of people setting out, mainly by sea, from Egypt and colonizing and civilizing the world. These merchant venturers of five thousand years ago were "the Children of the Sun."

But why, some people asked, did they set out on these extraordinary world travels? The answer given by Elliot Smith was in terms of the Givers of Life formula, and we had best give it here in his own words. "In delving into the remotely distant history of our species," he wrote in *The Evolution of the Dragon,*

> *we cannot fail to be impressed with the persistence with which, throughout the whole of his career, man . . . has been seeking . . . for an elixir of life to give added "vitality" to the dead . . . to prolong the days of active life to the living, to restore growth and to protect his own life from all assaults, not merely of time but also of circumstance.*

These world travelers were then, according to Elliot Smith and Perry, looking for elixirs, for what they called collectively "givers of life." They set out from Egypt and reached almost everywhere. There was no civilization before Egypt, at least no civilization that was not derived from Egypt. Elliot Smith immediately crossed swords with ethnologists in America because to him the Central American civilizations were certainly derived from Egypt. Everything started in Egypt—everything. When he was once asked what was taking place in the cultural development of the world when Egypt was allegedly laying the foundations of civilization, he answered at once "Nothing." Perry's comment on this statement is flabbergasting in its naivety and ignorance. "The accumulation of fresh evidence during the twenty-odd years that have since elapsed has tended to confirm the essential accuracy of what was then an astonishing generalization." Those are Perry's very words; at least we can be in agreement with the phrase "astonishing generalization."

We do not want to spend too long in discussing the authors of this pan-Egyptian hyperdiffusion theory. Elliot Smith and Perry really abandoned any pretense at scientific method. They did not evaluate the evidence and arrive at a theory. Elliot Smith had been swept away by Egypt, he had been convinced by mummies and megaliths, his theory was formed and everything was squeezed into this theory —circumstances of time, place, and function were brushed aside with airy condescension. Lowie[2] is not a whit too sharp, not an iota too cruel when he says of the astonishing development of the Elliot Smith theories:

> Here there is no humble quest of the truth, no patient scrutiny of difficulties, no attempt to understand sincere criticism. Vehement reiteration takes the place of argument. . . . Everything is grist for his mill, everything is either black or white. . . . In physical anthropology Elliot Smith controls the facts hence, right or wrong—his judgments command respect while in ethnography his crass ignorance darkens counsel.

Nor is Lowie too severe when he refers to "the unfathomable ignorance of elementary ethnography" displayed by Elliot Smith and Perry. In a lecture on *Conversion in Science* which Elliot Smith gave

[2] Robert H. Lowie (1883–1957) was an American anthropologist who taught for thirty-three years at the University of California at Berkeley. A very productive scholar, his personal bibliography totals about 400 separate pieces of writing. Most of his writings were on ethnology.—Ed.

in 1928 at the Imperial College of Science—it was the Huxley Memorial Lecture—he said this: "The set attitude of mind of a scholar may become almost indistinguishable from a delusion." He was not, quite naturally, thinking of himself when he wrote this sentence, but this is unfortunately just what had happened to him. He had acquired a set attitude of mind with regard to the Egyptian origin of all culture, and it had become a delusion.

To us at the present day it is a distraction to look back at this pan-Egyptian diffusionist delusion but its significance is much more than an amusing sidelight on the development of ideas of prehistory. For the Elliot Smith–Perry school were not alone in their search for a simple all-embracing solution. Elliot Smith died in 1937. Two years later Lord Raglan published his *How Came Civilization*. Raglan is still with us and writing but he corresponds in his essential philosophical basis with Elliot Smith and Perry. He does not believe in the possibility of inventions being made twice. Let us quote his views.

No invention, discovery, custom, belief, or even story is known for certain to have originated in two separate cultures. . . . The natural state of man is a state of low savagery . . . towards that state he always tends to revert whenever he is not checked, or forced in the opposite direction, by that unexplained, but highly artificial localized and spasmodic process which we know as the progress of civilization . . . savages never invent or discover anything . . . many of the principal discoveries and inventions upon which our civilization is based can be traced with considerable probability to an area with its focus near the head of the Persian Gulf, and such evidence as there is suggests that they were made by ingenious priests as a means of facilitating the performance of religious ritual.

Lord Raglan allows a great civilizing process to take place in the sixteenth century A.D. but this is only the second time in man's whole history, and his general conclusion remains that "civilization then, far from being a process that keeps going on everywhere, is really an event which has only happened twice." Raglan has done little more than substitute Sumeria for Egypt. . . .

Now why does the world tolerate this academic rubbish from people like Elliot Smith, Perry, and Raglan? There are many reasons. First there is a deep-seated desire for a simple answer to complicated problems. That is why the earlier pre-archaeological prehistorians clutched at the Trojans, the Phoenicians, the Lost Tribes of Israel, the Druids, and, let us particularly not forget in this present

context, the Egyptians. The Ancient Egyptians as the saviors of the
world were invented long before Elliot Smith was made Professor of
Anatomy in Cairo. And this simplistic easy solution to prehistory is
still something which people hanker after. I have little doubt that the
cult of Atlantis at the present day is a part of this, and the sale of
books explaining how all civilization came from the vanished island
of Atlantis, or Mu, or Lake Titicaca, or Heligoland is a proof of it.
These theories are still widely canvassed at the present day and the
books dealing with them sell well, and one is always being asked
about Atlantis and Titicaca just as one is asked about Phoenicians
and the Lost Tribes of Israel.

It is often said by professional archaeological scholars that we
should not concern ourselves unduly with what is after all only one
aspect of the rather large lunatic fringe of prehistory, that we have
far better things to do advancing the true path of knowledge and accumulating by archaeological means the basic facts to be distilled
out of prehistory, and that most of these extraordinary books giving
single origins to man's civilization in one great movement or event
or spread of culture-heroes are beneath contempt. There is much in
this, but here we *are* concerned with the ideas people have or want
to have about prehistory, and there is no doubt that many have had
and want to have the simple solutions of an Elliot Smith, a Raglan,
a Bellamy, or a Spanuth. This is not merely because, as I have said,
there seems a deep-seated desire for a simple all-embracing explanation but because the gradual elaboration and complication of the
archaeological record has begun to bewilder people. It was all right
in Victorian times when you could read Lubbock's *Prehistoric Times*[3]
or in Edwardian times when you read Rice Holmes's *Ancient Britain
and the Invasions of Julius Caesar,*[4] all right when the prehistoric
past of man seemed an easily assimilable tale of Palaeolithic, Neolithic, Bronze Age, and Early Iron Age, but not all right when you began to read the complicated story which prehistorians offer at the
present day with its extraordinarily complicated sequences of cultures
in different areas. Look for example at any chart at the end of

[3] Sir John Lubbock (1834–1913) was an English biologist, anthropologist, and popular writer on science. A close friend of Charles Darwin, Lubbock became an ardent
supporter of Darwin's theory of evolution as is evidenced in his most influential
work, *The Origin of Civilization and the Primitive Condition of Man* (1870).—Ed.
[4] Thomas Rice Edward Holmes (1855–1933) was a British classical scholar, noted
for his authoritative works on ancient Britain, Gaul, and Julius Caesar.—Ed.

Childe's *Dawn of European Civilization*[5] or of Christopher Hawkes's *Prehistoric Foundations of Europe*, at the chart at the end of Stuart Piggott's *Neolithic Cultures of the British Isles*, and you may well be pardoned if you recoil from the complicated archaeological constructs which seem to have replaced the simple succession which the Victorians so gladly elaborated. . . .

It is then we suggest, as part of a desire for a simple all-embracing solution, and as part of a reaction from the complexity of the archaeological record, that we should look at the distractions of this hyperdiffusionism which beset the fringes of our discipline. . . .

It needs emphasizing here that the error lies in the simplistic hyperdiffusion of the one-center school, just as the Victorian unilinear system of cultural evolution was an error. Neither diffusion nor evolution itself as an explanation of cultural change is an error; the error has lain in the extravagant interpretation of cultural change in terms of only one of these explanations and that taken to obsessional extremes. In the new prehistory which was coming into being in the twenties diffusion was the accepted explanation of cultural change in archaeology. The man who was perhaps most responsible for slowly and surely putting across a modified diffusionism was Gordon Childe in his *Dawn of European Civilization* (1925), his *Danube in Prehistory* (1929), and his *Bronze Age* (1930). In these books we see developing the climate of the new prehistory which carefully builds up the details of the succession of cultures in each area and sees cultures or elements of cultures spreading from one area to another. This diffusionism is not open to the charges leveled—and very correctly—at the hyperdiffusionist school, namely that it neglected all semblance of scientific methods.

In our own modern prehistory the Childe and Childe-derivative archaeologists are working in the best traditions of scientific method. Before two cultural objects or traditions are compared it is made certain that they are functionally and formally identical. It is one of the great confusions of the Elliot Smith–Perry school of hyperdiffusion that they never made sure that the objects they were comparing were functionally and formally identical; they rashly compared the Pyra-

[5] Vere Gordon Childe (1892–1957), an Australian prehistorian, pioneered in the systematic study of European prehistory of the third and second milleniums, and showed how technological advances marked the birth of human civilization. Childe's views will be more fully explored in the following selection.—Ed.

mids of Egypt with the Pyramids of Central America, monuments which are admittedly superficially identical, without realizing that while the Egyptian pyramids were tombs, the American pyramids were great temple platforms on the top of which religious rites were performed. The diffusionists of the new prehistory do not make these mistakes; they compare only cultural features which are formally and functionally identical and only derive the one from the other if such a historical process can be shown to be chronologically, geographically, and historically possible.

Let me take as an example of the modified Childe diffusionism of the twenties, which had become standard archaeological theory in the thirties and forties, the megalithic tombs of western Europe. In the nineteenth century the likenesses between megalithic tombs from Denmark and the Orkneys[6] to Iberia and the Mediterranean were appreciated, but there then seemed only one of two possible explanations for these likenesses. The first was that these monuments had come into existence naturally in different areas as part of the natural cultural evolution of man. The second view was that there was a great megalithic master race which spread from one center—Denmark itself was sometimes canvassed, and at other times it was some unspecified area in the east Mediterranean—indeed at the present day the general view is to talk in fairly vague terms of an Aegean or Minoan–Mycenaean cultural spread. We have already seen how Elliot Smith and Perry took over this idea of a megalithic race which became part of their pan-Egyptian colonial movement.

But when one gets down to detailed analysis of the spread of megalithic tombs in the western Mediterranean and western Europe, one sees that no one facile explanation will suffice. In the first place megaliths do not represent a single unitary movement but contacts along the same routes over many centuries. Many scholars at the present day would date the first passage graves of Ireland and Brittany to the middle of the third millennium B.C., but it is equally clear to many who look at the decorated entrance slab at New Grange that it must be compared with the spirals and lozenges on the blocking slabs at Castelluccio in Sicily, the Hal Tarxien slabs in Malta, and the designs on the shaft-graves at Mycenae—all evidence of contact across Europe in the sixteenth or fifteenth century B.C. Secondly,

[6] A cluster of islands, 376 square miles in area, off the northeast coast of Scotland. —Ed.

even if one allows initial movements of people with a basic tomb type and a basic custom of collective burial, that basic tomb type is probably a rock-cut tomb; megalithic architecture may have arisen independently in the west Mediterranean in several places, Malta for instance and southern Spain and southern France. Tomb types in these separate areas developed often along parallel lines.

There has been in recent years an even greater revolution in the generally accepted modified Childe diffusionism. Northern antiquaries have for a long time classified the megalithic tombs of Denmark, Sweden, and Germany into three successive groups, first the *dös* or *dysse* usually confusingly translated into English as "dolmen" —a word used in English in a very wide variety of ways; secondly the passage grave, and thirdly the long stone cist. Now while at first it was argued that these three stages represented a simple evolutionary sequence in northern Europe, the later diffusionist view was that each stage represented a movement from some part of western Europe and the west Mediterranean. The last stage characterized by the long stone cists was thought, for instance, to have spread from the Paris basin somewhere between 1600 and 1400 B.C. and this is still a possibility; the second stage characterized by passage graves was, and indeed still is, seen as part of the spread of passage graves in western Europe between 2500 and 1500 B.C. The first stage, that characterized by *dösar, dysser,* or *dolmens,* was less easily explained but there were vague parallels to these monuments in western Europe—various archaeologists pointed hopefully, if a little uncertainly, at the polygonal dolmens of Portugal and the rectangular dolmens of the Pyrenean area. But now as the result of detailed researches by Professor Becker of Copenhagen we see the tombs of this first stage as something quite different, as the translation into megalithic architecture of earth graves that existed in northern Europe before; what is more, Professor Becker reminds us that these first-stage megalithic tombs are not collective tombs at all and never contained more than a few burials. It now looks as though we must accept the independent origin of some megalithic architecture in Denmark.

Very gradually we are entering on a new mid-twentieth-century stage in our ideas of the interpretation of prehistoric change: indeed after the distractions of the hyperdiffusionists and the fairly generally accepted reasonable doctrine of the modified diffusionists we are back to one of the Victorian positions when, said Lowie, as I have already quoted, "evolution . . . lay down amicably beside Diffusion."

There is now, then, a very considerable change going on in the view which people are beginning to have and express about the nature of cultural spread and change in prehistory. Yet some would say that while we may be forced to modify our views in detail on some points the overall picture is the same. The overall picture would appear to be something like this: that the elements of a higher food-producing civilization came into existence in the Near East in and around what Breasted[7] called the Fertile Crescent, and that the elements of this culture complex spread all over the world, not of course diffused by a master race, but by varying peoples in varying stages. Perhaps there were two great stages, the earliest of which was called by Childe the Neolithic Revolution of, perhaps, ten thousand years ago, and the second the Urban Revolution of five thousand years ago which produced urban literate communities in Egypt and Mesopotamia. This was the picture painted in Gordon Childe's *What Happened in History* and *Man Makes Himself,* and in the series of books written by H. J. E. Peake and H. J. Fleure called *The Corridors of Time.* The first volume of *The Corridors of Time* was published under the title *Apes and Men* in 1927, and the tenth and last volume, called *Times and Places,* in 1956; Peake had himself died in 1946. Now Peake and Fleure were not Elliot Smith–Perry diffusionists, indeed Peake used to say with a twinkle that he found it difficult to look at the world through a Perryscope. But the Peake and Fleure books on which my generation of archaeologists was brought up, admirably demonstrate the modified Childe diffusionism of the twenties and thirties.

Let me quote from the preface to the last volume, *Times and Places.*

> It has been the writers' belief in compiling the Corridors that southwest Asia was the region in which man made the great step forward from dependence on hunting and collecting to food-production by cereal cultivation; and to this the keeping of domestic animals was soon added. While there may have been small attempts at cultivation begun independently elsewhere, and there were probably several more or less

---

[7] James Henry Breasted (1865–1935) established the study of Egyptology in the United States and became the foremost authority in this field. His *History of Egypt* (1905) was the first scholarly history of the ancient Nile written in the United States. —Ed.

independent beginnings of the domestication of animals, the spread of food-production from southwest Asia and Egypt and its consequences remain major features of the story of mankind.

Now this is very true, but how major is another story which Peake and Fleure omit entirely from their ten-volume essay down the corridors of time, and this omission is deliberate and planned. "The Americas," they write, "with their largely distinct problems have not been included in the survey." But the problem of prehistory is the problem of the prehistory of man, not the prehistory of the Old World. We find the same refusal to study the American evidence in Gordon Childe's *What Happened in History*. Yet the story of New World cultural origins is of paramount importance to our study of Old World cultural origins.

The Western World learned about the Americas for the first time in 1492 when Christopher Columbus discovered America when looking for the Indies. The subsequent explorers of Central America "succeeded in doing," to quote Carleton Coon's words, "something every archaeologist dreams of which is to step backwards in time . . . they marched into an Early Metal Age civilization comparable in many respects with that of Egypt in late Predynastic or early Dynastic times, and that of earliest Sumeria." Since then historians and archaeologists have wanted to find out how this civilization came into existence and what relation it bore to the civilizations of the ancient world. The Spanish found themselves in the New World face to face with the Aztecs of Mexico who met them in battle with composite weapons of obsidian blades set in grooved wood, and the Mayas of Yucatan, Guatemala, and the Honduras who built elaborate temples and pyramids and who had no metal at all except a few gold and copper ornaments, and the Incas of Peru who had complicated networks of roads like the Roman roads, suspension bridges of rope, and domesticated animals—the llama, the alpaca, and the guinea-pig. All these three native American civilizations—Aztecs, Mayas, and Incas—were based on agriculture. And both the Aztecs and Mayas as well as other American Indians in Mexico could write; they had a pictographic script which they wrote in deerskin books.

How had all this come about? Of course Christopher Columbus was not the first European to visit America. Leif Ericsson got to Greenland and Vinland in A.D. 1001. It is not suggested that Leif

Ericsson introduced the elements of higher civilization to America, but it has been the fashion to suggest that someone did do this, and, of course, particularly the fashion by those who could not bring themselves to believe that anything could be invented or discovered on more than one occasion. While there has been a fashion, there has been no agreement on who brought (or was thought to have brought) the higher civilization to America. To some they were Phoenicians or the Lost Tribes of Israel, to others Welshmen like Madoc or Irishmen like St. Brandon, to other Negroes from Africa, Japanese, Polynesians, or people from the supposed and supposedly sunken continents of Atlantis, Lemuria, or Mu—or of course if you were looking at prehistory through a Perryscope, it was brought by the ancient Egyptians themselves. . . .

That may be so, but in studying American cultural origins we are engaged in what is almost a controlled laboratory experiment. That is why American prehistory is so important to the prehistorian working in Europe or the Near East or India. We are now in a position to give objective answers to American prehistoric chronology—answers based first on dendrochronological[8] researches but latterly on Carbon-14 analysis. The Carbon-14 dates in the Bat Cave in New Mexico show that American Indians were growing maize by 4000 B.C. Further comparative analysis and study shows that almost every cultural element in the New World can be explained as of purely local growth. There are still some puzzles—the gourd, cotton, the sweet potato, and Indian corn are among them—but on the whole the story as it looks at this moment is that about 10,000 B.C. man came to America probably across a dry Bering Straits, and that by 5000 B.C. all of the New World except the Eskimo country was occupied. By 4000 B.C. agriculture had begun in the New World and in due course these early agricultural communities developed into the Urban Civilizations of Central America; and at the moment it looks as though this development happened in America without any contact of a serious nature from abroad. It was in fact a tale of independent cultural evolution.

If this was so in America, we now ask, why not elsewhere in the Old World? Rice cultivation probably developed independently in south China when wheat and barley were being cultivated in the Near East and maize in America. Indeed it is probably true that we

---

[8] Dendrochronology is the study of the growth rings in trees to determine the date of past events.—Ed.

have been creating our own difficulties to a certain extent, and inventing the problems of diffusion versus local evolution by conceptualizing certain ideas. Agriculture and civilization are two such ideas; we talk about the origins of "agriculture" and discuss whether "it" started in the Near East and spread from there to China, India, and America when all the time what we should be talking about is the discovery of the cultivation of wheat and barley in Egypt, Palestine, and Iraq, of rice in eastern India and south China, and of maize and squash in Central America. We have created our own problems by grouping together all these material advances in culture under one word, "agriculture." And it is to a certain extent the same with "civilization." We describe civilizations in Egypt, Sumeria, the Indus Valley, China, and Central America and ask how they came into existence, flourished, and decayed, and what was their genetic interrelationship—without perhaps realizing that because all these societies had writing and cities and a high skill in metalworking they are not necessarily connected.

It would seem, then, that we have traveled a long way from the earlier diffusionists to our present very modified diffusionism with its recognition of the real existence of independent evolution; perhaps that long way had to involve the distractions of the hyperdiffusionists. I said in the previous lectures, that the development of the prehistoric record had brought us to a stage where we were studying the development of cultures in time and space, that we were studying a gaily colored layer cake. The first concern of prehistoric archaeology was the study of the chronological and spatial position of these layers. It was also, secondarily, the study of their interrelations if the time-space positions permitted such interrelationships; this study, which after all is the only way in which we can begin to understand cultural change and its complex mechanics, is one we should undertake without any preconceived ideas of diffusion and independent invention.

We should approach this study of cultural origins and change at the present day with the lessons of American prehistory very much in mind, for here it does seem that man developed from the Mesolithic food-gathering savages of the end of the Ice Age through to the literate urban communities of Central America without significant contacts observable in the archaeological record from the Old World of Europe and Africa on the one hand or Asia and Indonesia on the other. If there is one lesson more than any other which mid-twentieth-century research is forcibly injecting into our idea of prehistory it is that of the independent development of prehistoric American culture. The news of the early dating by Carbon-14 of the first American agricultural communities has come like a tremendous blast of cold wind blowing down the corridors of time where walked scholars who seemed to have arrived at a fixed picture of world prehistory and cultural origins in terms of Neolithic and Urban Revolutions in the Near East.

III CIVILIZATION: MAN MAKES HIMSELF

V. Gordon Childe

MATERIAL PROGRESS AND THE ADVENT OF CIVILIZATION

A paragon in prehistoric scholarship over the last century was V. Gordon Childe. A native Australian, Childe graduated from Sydney and Oxford Universities and served as the first Abercromby Professor of Prehistoric Archaeology at the University of Edinburg. The seminal ideas emitted from his works have influenced an international host of scholars. A doctrinaire Marxist, Childe concluded that the advent of civilization was the result of two revolutions: "the neolithic and urban revolutions." These revolutions, and consequently civilization, were made possible in the Near East by a series of technological-economic changes that gave man mastery over his environment and freed a segment of the populace to acquire specialization. In the "Childe thesis" human progress takes precedent over organic evolution in explaining the advent of civilization. Childe's Man Makes Himself *was first published in 1936.*

It has been suggested that prehistory is a continuation of natural history, that there is an analogy between organic evolution and progress in culture. Natural history traces the emergence of new species each better adapted for survival, more fitted to obtain food and shelter, and so to multiply. Human history reveals man creating new industries and new economies that have furthered the increase of his species and thereby vindicated its enhanced fitness.

The wild sheep is fitted for survival in a cold mountain climate by its heavy coat of hair and down. Men can adapt themselves to life in the same environment by making coats out of sheeps' skin or of wool. With claws and snouts rabbits can dig themselves burrows to provide shelter against cold and enemies. With picks and shovels men can excavate similar refuges, and even build better ones out of brick, stone, and timber. Lions have claws and teeth with which to secure the meat they need. Man makes arrows and spears for slaying his game. An innate instinct, an inherited adjustment of its rudimentary nervous system, enables even the lowly jellyfish to grasp prey that is actually within its reach. Men learn more efficient and

Excerpted from chapters 2, 6, and 9 of *Man Makes Himself,* by V. Gordon Childe. Reprinted by permission of the publishers, Messrs. C. A. Watts.

discriminating methods of obtaining nourishment through the precept and example of their elders.

In human history, clothing, tools, weapons, and traditions take the place of fur, claws, tusks, and instincts in the quest for food and shelter. Customs and prohibitions, embodying centuries of accumulated experience and handed on by social tradition, take the place of inherited instincts in facilitating the survival of our species.

There certainly is an analogy. But it is essential not to lose sight of the significant distinctions between historical progress and organic evolution, between human culture and the animal's bodily equipment, between the social heritage and the biological inheritance. Figurative language, based on the admitted analogy, is liable to mislead the unwary. We read, for instance: "In the Jurassic epoch the struggle for life must have been very severe. . . . *Triceratops* covered its head and neck with a kind of bony bonnet with two horns over the eyes." The passage suggests the sort of thing that happens conspicuously in wartime. Between 1915 and 1918, finding themselves threatened from the air, the belligerents devised shrapnel-helmets, antiaircraft guns, bombproof shelters, and other protective contrivances. Now that process of invention is not in the least like the evolution of *Triceratops* as conceived by the biologists. Its bony bonnet was part of its body; it was inherited from its parents; it had been developed very slowly as a result of small spontaneous modifications in reptiles' body-covering that had been accumulating over hundreds of generations. It survived not because *Triceratops* liked it, but because those of his ancestors who possessed its rudiments had in actual practice succeeded better in acquiring food and eluding dangers than those that lacked this bodily equipment and protection. Man's equipment and defenses are external to his body; he can lay them aside and don them at will. Their use is not inherited, but learned, rather slowly, from the social group to which each individual belongs. Man's social heritage is a tradition which he begins to acquire only after he has emerged from his mother's womb. Changes in culture and tradition can be initiated, controlled, or delayed by the conscious and deliberate choice of their human authors and executors. An invention is not an accidental mutation of the germ plasm, but a new synthesis of the accumulated experience to which the inventor is heir by tradition only. It is well to be as clear as possible as to the sort of differences subsisting between the processes here compared.

The mechanism of evolution as conceived by biologists need not be described in detail. It has been outlined elsewhere in accessible and readable books by experts. The current view seems to be briefly something like this. The evolution of new forms of life and of new species among animals is supposed to result from the accumulation of hereditable changes in the germ plasm. (The exact nature of these changes is as obscure to scientists as are the words germ plasm to the ordinary reader.) Such changes as facilitated the life and reproduction of the creature would become established by what is termed "natural selection." The creatures not affected by the changes in question would simply die out or become confined to some corner, leaving the new species in possession of the field. A concrete and partly fictitious example will illustrate the meaning better than several pages more of abstract terms.

About half a million years ago Europe and Asia were visited by periods of intense cold—the so-called Ice Ages—that lasted thousands of years. By that time there were in existence several species of elephant ancestral to modern African and Indian elephants. To meet the rigors of the Ice Age some elephants developed a shaggy coat of hair, becoming eventually what we term mammoths. This statement does not mean [that] an ordinary elephant said one day, "I feel horribly chilly; I will put on a shaggy coat," nor yet that by continually wishing for a coat it mysteriously made hairs to sprout out of its hide. What is supposed to have happened would be more like this:

The germ plasm is liable to change, and is constantly changing. Among the elephant calves born as the Ice Age was becoming severe were some that, as result of such a change in the germ plasm, were born with a tendency to hairy skins, and as they grew up actually became hairy. In the cold latitudes the hairy elephants would thrive better and rear larger families, also hairy, than the more normal type. They would accordingly increase at the expense of the rest. Moreover, similar mysterious changes in the germ plasm might result in some of their offspring being still more hairy than their ancestors and other contemporaries. These in their turn, being the best fitted to endure the cold, would thrive better and multiply faster than any others. And so, after many generations, a breed of hairy elephants or mammoths would be established as the result of the accumulation of the successive hereditary variations described. And such alone would be able to withstand the glacial conditions of northern Europe and Asia. The mammoth thus got his permanent shaggy coat, but as the result of a process extending over many generations and thousands of years—for elephants of all species are slow breeders.

During the Ice Ages several species of man already existed, contemporary with the mammoth: they hunted the beasts and drew pictures of them in caves. But they did not inherit shaggy coats and did not develop such to meet the crisis; some of the human inhabitants of Europe during the Ice Age would pass unrecognized in a crowd today. Instead of undergoing the slow physical changes which eventually enable the mammoths to endure the cold, our ancestors found out how to control fire and to make coats out of skins. And so they were able to face the cold as successfully as the mammoths.

Of course, while the mammoth-calf was born with a tendency to a hairy coat, which inevitably grew as the calf matured, the human infant was not born as a fire tender or coat maker. The parent mammoths transmitted their coats to their progeny by heredity. Each generation of human children had to be taught the whole art of keeping fires going and making coats from the very rudiments. The art was transmitted from parent to child only by precept and example. It was an "acquired characteristic," and acquired characteristics, zoologists agree, are not hereditary. An infant by himself on his natal day is no more a fire tender than when, half a million years ago, man first began to cherish the flames instead of fleeing from them like other beasts. . . .

Both men and mammoths were successfully adjusted to the environment of the Ice Ages. Both flourished and multiplied under those peculiar climatic conditions. But their ultimate histories diverged. The last Ice Age passed, and with its passage the mammoth became extinct. Man has survived. The mammoth was too well adapted to a particular set of conditions; it was overspecialized. When, with the onset of more temperate conditions, forests covered the wide tundras on which the mammoth had roamed and temperate vegetation replaced the Arctic scrub on which the mammoth browsed, the beast was helpless. The bodily characters—hairy coat, digestive system adjusted to consume dwarf willows or mosses, hoofs and trunk constructed for rooting in the snow—which had enabled him to thrive in the Ice Ages, all proved to be handicaps in temperate climates. Man, on the other hand, was free to leave off his coat if he was too hot, to invent other tools, and to choose beef instead of mammoth steaks. . . .

In the comparatively short evolutionary history documented by fossil remains, man has not improved his inherited equipment by bodily changes detectable in his skeleton. Yet he has been able to adjust himself to a greater range of environments than almost any other creature, to multiply infinitely faster than any near relative among the higher mammals, and to beat the polar bear, the hare, the hawk, and the tiger at their special tricks. Through his control of fire and the skill to make clothes and houses, man can, and does, live and thrive from the Arctic Circle to the Equator. In the trains and cars he builds, man can outstrip the fleetest hare or ostrich. In airplanes he can mount higher than the eagle, and with telescopes see farther than the hawk. With firearms he can lay low animals that a tiger dare not tackle.

But fire, clothes, houses, trains, airplanes, telescopes and guns are not, we must repeat, part of man's body. He can leave them and lay them aside at will. They are not inherited in the biological sense, but the skill needed for their production and use is part of our social heritage, the result of a tradition accumulated over many generations, and transmitted, not in the blood, but through speech and writing. . . .

The evolution of man's body, of his physiological equipment, is studied by prehistoric anthropology, a branch of paleontology. Beyond the points already considered, its results have little bearing upon the subject of this book. Within our species improvements in the equipment which men make for themselves—i.e., in culture—have taken the place of bodily modifications. Prehistoric anthropology does not at present even dispose of concrete documents that illustrate accurately the evolutionary processes that must be regarded as necessary preliminaries to the intelligent creation of culture. None of the rare fossil "men" whose skeletons have survived from the earlier (pleistocene) Ice Ages can be classed among our direct ancestors. They do not represent stages in Nature's process of man-making, but abortive experiments—genera and species—that have died out. . . .

It is archaeology that studies progress in culture. Its documents are the tools, weapons, and huts that men of the past made in order to secure food and shelter. They illustrate improving technical skill, accumulating knowledge, and advancing organization for securing a livelihood. Obviously a finished tool, fashioned by human hands, is a good gauge of the manual dexterity of its maker. Rather less obviously is it the measure of the scientific knowledge of his period. Yet any tool does really reflect, albeit rather imperfectly, the science at the disposal of its makers. That is really self-evident in the case of a wireless valve or an airplane. It is equally true of a bronze axe, but a word of explanation may be useful.

Archaeologists have divided the cultures of the past into Stone Ages (Old and New), Bronze Age, and Iron Age, on the basis of the material generally and by preference employed for cutting implements. Bronze axes and knives are tools distinctive of a Bronze Age as contrasted with stone ones, indicating an earlier Stone Age, or iron ones, marking the subsequent Iron Age. Now a great deal more science has to be applied in the manufacture of a bronze ax than in making a stone one. The former implies a quite considerable working knowledge of geology (to locate and identify the ores) and chemistry (to reduce them), as well as the mastery of complicated technical processes. A "Stone Age" folk, using exclusively stone implements, presumably lacked that knowledge. So the criteria used by archaeologists to distinguish his several "ages" serve also as indexes to the state of science.

But when the tools, hut-foundations, and other archaeological remains of a given age and locality are considered not in isolation, but in their totality, they may reveal much more. They disclose not only the level of technical skill and science attained, but also the manner in which their makers got their livelihood, their economy. And it is this economy which determines the multiplication of our species, and so its biological success. Studied from this angle, the old archaeological divisions assume a new significance. The archaeologist's ages correspond roughly to economic stages. Each new "age" is ushered in by an economic revolution of the same kind and having the same effect as the "Industrial Revolution" of the eighteenth century.

In the "Old Stone Age" (paleolithic period) men relied for a living entirely on hunting, fishing, and gathering wild berries, roots, slugs, and shellfish. Their numbers were restricted by the provision of food made for them by Nature, and seem actually to have been very small. In the "New Stone Age" (neolithic times) men control their own food supply by cultivating plants and breeding animals. Given favorable circumstances, a community can now produce more food than it needs to consume, and can increase its production to meet the requirements of an expanding population. A comparison of the number of burials from the Old Stone Age with that from the New in Europe and the Near East shows that, as a result of the neolithic revolution, the population had increased enormously. From the biological standpoint the new economy was a success; it had made possible a multiplication of our species. . . .

* * *

The neolithic revolution, just described, was the climax of a long process. It has to be presented as a single event because archaeology can only recognize the result; the several steps leading up thereto are beyond the range of direct observation. A second revolution transformed some tiny villages of self-sufficing farmers into populous cities, nourished by secondary industries and foreign trade, and regularly organized as States. Some of the episodes which ushered in this transformation can be discerned, if dimly, by prehistory. The scene of the drama lies in the belt of semi-arid countries between the Nile and the Ganges. Here epoch-making inventions seem to have followed one another with breathless speed, when we recall the slow pace of progress in the millennia before the first revolution or even in the four millennia between the second and the Industrial Revolution of modern times.

Between 6000 and 3000 B.C. man has learnt to harness the force of oxen and of winds, he invents the plow, the wheeled cart, and the sailboat, he discovers the chemical processes involved in smelting copper ores and the physical properties of metals, and he begins to work out an accurate solar calendar. He has thereby equipped himself for urban life, and prepares the way for a civilization which shall require writing, processes of reckoning, and standards of measurement—instruments of a new way of transmitting knowledge and of exact sciences. In no period of history till the days of Galileo was progress in knowledge so rapid or far-reaching discoveries so frequent.

The neolithic revolution left the whole area from the Nile and the East Mediterranean across Syria and Iraq to the Iranian plateau and to the Indus valley beyond sprinkled with neolithic communities. It may be assumed that great diversity in culture reigned throughout this vast zone, just as it does today. We may suspect many scattered groups of hunters and fishers, survivals of the pre-neolithic economy, migratory horticulturists, and still more nomadic pastoralists. But none of these communities is as yet directly known; archaeologists have concentrated their attention upon more settled communities, upon the sites of villages which have often grown into cities. Even these exhibit great diversity in crafts, in art, and in general economy, but a few abstract traits are common to all.

The populations are essentially sedentary. The favored sites remain continuously occupied right into historical times. Daughter colonies may be planted as the community grows, but as far as possible the village itself expanded till it became a town. The geographical and economic factors favoring permanent settlement can easily be guessed.

In the first place, really desirable sites are limited in a zone of countries which were becoming increasingly arid and afflicted with ever worse droughts. Permanent water supplies—perennial springs and streams that would supply the needs of large assemblages of men and livestock, and supplement the scanty rainfall by irrigating fields and gardens—were diminishing. As the human race multiplied under the stimulus of the first revolution, such became rare and valuable possessions.

Then the profitable exploitation of these natural oases was a particularly laborious task requiring the collective effort of a large body of workers. Precisely as the ultimate yield in food-stuffs was to be abundant, so the preliminary exertions in preparing the land were heavy and irksome. The Nile, whose annual flood provides both water and soil, offered a certain and abundant livelihood. But the valley bottom that is reached by the flood was originally a series of swamps and reedy jungles. Its reclamation was a stupendous task: the swamps had to be drained by channels, the violence of floodwaters to be restrained by banks, the thicket to be cleared away, the wild beasts lurking in them to be exterminated. No small group could hope to make headway against such obstacles. It needed a strong force capable of acting together to cope with recurrent crises that threatened drainage channels and banks. The few original patches of habitable and cultivable land had to be extended with sweat and blood. The soil, thus hardly conquered, was a sacred heritage; no one would willingly abandon fields so laboriously created. And there was no need to abandon them, since the river itself renewed their fertility every year.

Lower Mesopotamia, the region termed Sumer at the dawn of history, presented a like task. Between the main channels of the Tigris and the Euphrates was a vast tract of swamps, only recently raised by the river silt above the waters of the Persian Gulf. The swamps were covered with a tangle of gigantic reed-brakes interspersed with groves of date-palms. They were interrupted only by low ridges of rocky outcrop or banks of sandy silt. But they swarmed perpetually with animal life while on either side the steppes above flood level were parched and barren throughout the long blazing summer and the bitter winter. Attracted perhaps by the game, wild fowl, and fish, and by the groves of date-palms, the proto-Sumerians tackled the stupendous task of taming the Tigris-Euphrates delta and making it fit for habitation.

The land on which the great cities of Babylonia were to rise had literally to be created; the prehistoric forerunner of the biblical Erech was built on a sort of platform of reeds, laid crisscross upon the alluvial mud. The Hebrew book of Genesis has familiarized us with much older traditions of the pristine condition of Sumer—a "chaos" in which the boundaries between water and dry land were still fluid. An essential incident in "The Creation" is the separation of these elements. Yet it was no god, but the proto-Sumerians themselves who created the land; they dug channels to water the fields and drain the marsh; they built dikes and mounded platforms to protect men and cattle from the waters and raise them above the flood; they made the first clearings in the reed-brakes and explored the channels between them. The tenacity with which the memory of this struggle persisted in tradition is some measure of the exertion imposed upon the ancient Sumerians. Their reward was an assured supply of nourishing dates, a bounteous harvest from the fields they had drained, and permanent pastures for flocks and herds.

But they would naturally be attached to fields so laboriously won and to settlements so carefully protected: they would not willingly desert them to find new dwellings. And it was easier from the original mound and the nuclear clearing to extend the area of habitable land and cultivate mud than to found fresh settlements in the heart of the undrained swamp. Additional inhabitants were a positive advantage to a marsh village. With their labor, drainage channels could be extended and embankments enlarged to provide more land for cultivation and more room for settlement. Even more than in Upper Egypt, natural conditions in Sumer favored a large community and required organized social cooperation on an ever-increasing scale. But the same conditions must have prevailed also in the Nile Delta (as contrasted with the narrow valley above Cairo).

In adjacent regions—in the valleys of Syrian or Iranian torrents, for instance—conditions were rather less exacting. But even there permanent improvements had to be effected in the way of irrigation canals and drainage channels, and such would enhance the attraction of the site affected.

So all through the Near East the best sites were reclaimed with toil. Capital in the form of human labor was being sunk in the land. Its expenditure bound men to the soil; they would not lightly forgo the interest brought in by their reproductive works. And all the works in question were collective undertakings, they benefited the community as a whole, and were beyond the power of any individual. And generally their execution required capital in the form of a stock of surplus foodstuffs, accumulated by and at the disposal of the community. The workers engaged in draining and embanking must be fed; but while so employed they were not directly producing the food they consumed. As the reproductive works of a community became more ambitious, so the need for an accumulated stock of surplus foodstuffs would increase. Such an accumulation was a precondition of the growth of the village into a city, by conquering ever more of the territory surrounding it from marsh and desert.

Incidentally, conditions of life in a river valley or other oasis place in the hands of society an exceptional power for coercing its members; the community can refuse a recalcitrant access to water and can close the channels that irrigate his fields. Rain falleth upon the just and the unjust alike, but irrigating waters reach the fields by channels that the community has constructed. And what society has provided, society can also withdraw from the unjust and confine to the just alone. The social solidarity needed by irrigators can thus be imposed owing to the very circumstances that demand it. And young men cannot escape the restraint of their elders by founding fresh villages when all beyond the oasis is waterless desert. So when the social will comes to be expressed through a chief or a king, he is invested not merely with moral authority, but with coercive force too; he can apply sanctions against the disobedient.

A third stabilizing factor in the Near East was the enlargement of the farmer's diet: dates, figs, olives, and other fruits were added to barley and wheat-flour. Such fruits are nourishing and easy to preserve and transport. At first they would be gathered from wild trees. A grove of wild date-palms in Sumer or of fig-trees in Syria would enhance the value, and even determine the choice, of a site of settlement. Now fruit-trees go on bearing year after year, but are unmovable. To enjoy their fruits you must abide in their vicinity, or at least return to them every year.

And soon fruit-trees and vines were being cultivated. That, of course, involved an entirely new technique of husbandry. Men had to learn by experience the secrets of pruning for wood or for fruit, of grafting, and of artificial fertilization. The stages of this education are unknown, the beginnings of fruit-growing and viticulture have still to be elucidated. They certainly go back to prehistoric times. . . .

Sedentary life gave opportunities for improved housing accommodation and paved the way for architecture. The earliest Egyptian farmers had been content with simple wind-screens of reeds plastered with mud. The proto-Sumerians dwelt in tunnel-like houses of growing reeds or of mats hung upon bundles of reeds. But soon houses built of mud or *terre pisée* were being erected both in Egypt and in Asia. And long before 3000 B.C. the brick was invented in Syria or Mesopotamia. It is essentially just a lump of mud mixed with straw, that has been shaped by pressing into a wooden mold and then dried in the sun. But its invention made free construction and monumental architecture possible. . . .

The prosperous farmers settled in the oases and river valleys of the Near East appear to have been much more prone to surrender their economic self-sufficiency than the poor communities that in Europe are styled neolithic. Their readiness to make the sacrifice is a corollary of the variety of economies practiced in the area. As already remarked, besides the prosperous villages of settled farmers, communities of fishers, hunters, and seminomadic pastoralists must be assumed in the intervening spaces. Now the farming communities could easily produce more grain than was needed for home consumption. Very likely they would be glad to part with the surplus in exchange for fish, game, or pastoral products. And the poorer nomads, for their part, would be glad to barter their takings for corn. A certain interdependence between farming villages on the one hand and groups of fishers, hunters, or herdsmen on the other could very easily arise. Such interdependence exists today in a marked degree. The nomad Arab camel-breeders, for instance, depend for grain and manufactures upon settled cultivators. How early the economic specialization of different groups developed into that sort of interdependence is uncertain. It is presupposed in the earliest historical narratives; it may be inferred much earlier. The earliest Egyptian farmers had also been huntsmen, and their weapons were buried with them. In later graves, belonging to the same village, hunting implements are missing. One explanation for their absence would be that the later villagers found it more convenient to barter surplus farm produce for game than to hunt it themselves, as their forefathers had done.

Positive evidence for gradual breakdown of isolation is afforded by the increasing abundance of imported materials in prehistoric cemeteries and villages. Red Sea and Mediterranean shells have already been recorded in neolithic villages in Egypt. Rather later Egyptian graves contain in addition first malachite and resin, then also lapis lazuli and obsidian; later still amethysts and turquoise appear, and appear in increasing quantities. Now malachite must have been brought from Sinai or the East Desert of Nubia, resin from the forested mountains of Syria or Southern Arabia, obsidian from Melos in the Aegean, Arabia, Armenia, or possibly Abyssinia; lapis lazuli probably from the Iranian plateau.

In Sumer obsidian is found in the oldest settlements together with beads of amazonite that may have been brought from India or at least Armenia. In North Syria and Assyria obsidian was being imported as early as in Sumer, and lapis lazuli and turquoise soon appear. Foreign substances are found as imports very early also at Anau in Russian Turkestan and at Susa in Elam, east of the Tigris.

The transmission of foreign substances over such great distances in the Orient is best explained by the assumption of more mobile populations living alongside the permanent agricultural villages; it would indicate contact between the nomads and the farmers. In any case, it is the beginning of trade, the prerequisite of metallurgy.

The gems and semiprecious stones imported into Sumer and Egypt might be thought to be just luxuries, unessential adjuncts to the toilet. But that would probably be an incorrect judgment; very soon, in any case, these substances came to be regarded as necessities. The Egyptians used malachite for painting their eyelids, and a whole complex of devices grew up around it, as around tobacco-smoking with us. It was carried in richly ornamental leather pouches and ground up on palettes carved into the likeness of animals. The green color counteracted the sun's glare, and copper carbonate acted as a disinfectant against the eye diseases carried by flies in hot countries. But to the Egyptians these effects seemed magical; they valued malachite for the mystic property or *mana* resident in it. That is why its preparation was a ritual, why the pouches were decorated with amulets and the palettes carved into the shape of animals. It was the same with other "imports"—all were regarded as possessing some magic virtue. The cowrie shell resembles the vulva. To wear a cowrie therefore ensured fertility. The shell became a charm. The sanctity thus earned for it has made cowrie shells substitutes for money in parts of Africa and Asia. Native gold and the bright pebbles of the desert—carnelian, opal, and agate—as well as rarer stones, like turquoise and lapis, were again valued not only because they were pretty, but also because magic potencies reside in them. The magic virtues of jewels are frequently mentioned in ancient literatures, and the old ideas persisted throughout the Middle Ages even in Europe. Jewels were thus desired not as mere ornaments, but as practical means to the attainment of success, wealth, long life, offspring. From this standpoint they were not luxuries, but necessaries. . . .

The desire for gold, stones, and shells on account of magic properties supposedly resident in them had important practical consequences. It was a potent factor in breaking down the economic isolation of peasant communities. To obtain magic substances, needed to ensure the fertility of his fields and his own good luck, the thrifty peasant would be ready to part with grains and fruit to the nomads of the desert. To the latter, gems and malachite offered portable articles to barter for agricultural produce. Beads must have formed a staple of the earliest regular trade.

The high estimation of magic substances may well have led to an active search for them. For a later date W. J. Perry has envisaged a worldwide quest for gold, precious stones, amber, and other supposedly magical substances to have been undertaken by the Ancient Egyptians. It would have been a principal factor in the diffusion of civilization. Even though his contention must be regarded as exaggerated, the desire for such substances may well have prompted a sort of geological exploration of regions otherwise uninviting. And one fact is outstanding: malachite is a carbonate of copper, turquoise a phosphate of aluminum tinged with copper; and both occur in connection with copper ores; many of these ores are themselves brightly colored and presumably magical. The collection of malachite, turquoise, and other colored stones accordingly caused men to frequent metalliferous regions and put copper ores into their hands. To this extent the rise of metallurgy that was a dominant factor in the second revolution would be an indirect result of the magical ideas just considered.

Metalworking involved two groups or complexes of discoveries: (1) that copper, when hot, melts and can be cast into any desired shape, but on cooling becomes as hard, and will take on as good an edge, as stone, and (2) that the tough, trenchant, reddish metal can be produced by heating certain crystalline stones or earths in contact with charcoal. Copper, indeed, occurs naturally, though only rarely, in the metallic state as native copper. The pre-Columbian Indians of the Great Lakes region in U.S.A. utilized extensive local deposits of native copper for industrial ends. They treated the metal as a superior sort of stone, and even discovered its malleability, producing objects of beaten copper. But they never tried melting and casting it. Their procedures did not lead on to intelligent metallurgy, and it is unlikely that native copper played any significant part in the rise of the industry in the Old World. That depended from the outset on the reduction of copper ores.

The discovery involved might easily be made. A prehistoric Egyptian may have dropped some malachite on the glowing ashes of his hearth and seen the gleaming globules of metallic copper run out. A campfire, lit by some jewel-seeker in a metalliferous district against the outcrop of a surface lode, might reduce some of the ore. In the Katanga district prospectors have noticed beads of copper, thus accidentally smelted, among the ashes of Negroes' campfires. The reduction of copper might be discovered more than once, but its significance need not have been immediately appreciated. Small objects of copper—pins and even harpoon-heads—turn up sporadically in very early Egyptian graves. But they disclose no intelligent realization of the potentialities of metal. The copper has been hammered into thin rods, and bent or beaten into strips, and cut; it has, in fact, been subjected to the processes familiarly applied to bone, stone, and fibers—cutting, hammering, bending.

The real superiority of metal is that it is fusible and can be cast. Fusibility confers upon copper some of the merits of potter's clay. In working it the intelligent artificer is freed from the restrictions of size and shape imposed by bone or stone. A stone axe-head, a flint spear-point, or a bone harpoon can only be made by grinding, chipping, or cutting bits *off* the original piece. Molten copper is completely plastic, and will adapt itself to fill any desired form; it can be run into a mold of any shape and will assume, and on cooling retain, precisely the form outlined by the mold. The only limit to size is the capacity of the mold; you can run into it as much copper as you like. . . .

On the other hand, though so plastic when hot, the metal on cooling possesses the essential virtues of stone and bone; it is as solid, and will take as sharp an edge or as fine a point. Yet it has the additional advantage of being malleable. And finally, it is more permanent than stone or bone. A stone axe may easily be splintered by hard usage, and is then done for; at best its edge will often need regrinding, and it will soon be reduced to a useless size. But a copper axe can be remelted again and again, and will come out as good as new. The intelligent use of metal—let us say, simply metallurgy— begins when these advantages have been realized.

But that realization required a readjustment of the forms of thought. The change from tough solid copper to molten metal and back to the solid state again is dramatic, and must have seemed mysterious. The sameness between the shapeless lump of raw copper, the liquid in the crucible, and the well-formed casting, must at first have been difficult to grasp. Man was here controlling a remarkable process of physical change. He would have to adjust whatever naive ideas of substance he entertained in order to recognize identity through its several stages.

Moreover, the control of the process was only possible by means of a whole complex of discoveries and inventions. A temperature in the neighborhood of 1200° C is requisite to melt copper. That requires a blast. Some device had to be invented for forcing a current of air upon the flame; bellows are the correct solution, but are not directly attested till 1600 B.C. Furnaces, crucibles, and tongs had to be invented. Casting requires molds. It is easy enough to reproduce by casting an object that is flat on one side by impressing it on clay and pouring molten metal in the hollow left by the pattern. But that is useless for making a stout dagger with a ridge on both faces to strengthen it. Such an implement required a two-piece mold, the halves of which must correspond exactly and must be bound or clamped together. By 3000 B.C. the ingenious *cire perdue* process was employed in Mesopotamia. A model of the desired object is first made in wax and then coated in clay; the clay is heated, becoming pottery, while the wax is allowed to run out; metal is then poured into the cavity, and finally the clay mold is broken, disclosing the metal casting reproducing the form of the wax model.

These few words may suggest how intricate the course of casting really is. But the actual operations are much more tedious and intricate than a page of print can indicate. For instance, precautions must be taken to prevent the liquid metal from oxidizing or sticking to the mold. In a closed mold there is a danger of air bubbles forming, which would cause a fatal weakness in the casting. Again, after casting, the tool has to be hammered and smoothed down with a file or an abrasive.

Evidently the smith must dispose of a formidable body of industrial lore; his craft traditions embody the results of long experience and many deliberate experiments. They represent a new branch of applied science—elements carried over into modern chemistry and physics—but blended with a tangle of magic that we have happily forgotten. The transmission of this lore need not differ in kind from that of potter's lore. But the smith's task was more complicated and exacting than hers, the knowledge he required more specialized. It is very doubtful whether metallurgy could be practiced as a domestic industry in the intervals of agricultural work. Among modern barbarians smiths are normally specialists, and metalworking has probably always been a full-time job. The smith's may therefore be the oldest specialized craft save the magician's. But a community can afford a smith only if it possesses a surplus of foodstuffs; the smith, being withdrawn from food-production himself, must be fed from the unconsumed surplus of the farmers. The industrial use of metal may thus be treated as a sign of the specialization of labor, that a community's food supply exceeds its normal needs.

But it generally means more; it usually means the final sacrifice of economic independence. Copper is far from common; its ores are not found on the alluvial and löss plains preferred by neolithic farmers, but among wooded or stony ranges. Very few farming communities can have possessed copper mines on their home territory; the great majority had always to import the metal or its ore. In the end it had to be obtained by the production of a surplus of foodstuffs above what was needed for home consumption.

The scientific and economic implications of the extraction of metal from its ores are perhaps more far-reaching than those of metalworking. Copper ores are crystalline or powdery minerals generally occurring as veins in hard ancient rocks. The transformation of the ores into copper is a fairly simple chemical change. But what an astonishing one to early man! The ore does not look the least like the metal. The change it undergoes in contact with glowing carbon is miraculous—surely a change of substance, a transsubstantiation! The recognition of a continuity of substance must have been very difficult, and a rational account was achieved only by modern chemistry; till then alchemical ideas about transmutation could subsist. But, whatever his theories, man learned enough practical chemistry to distinguish what sorts of stone would yield copper when heated with carbon.

The right sorts of stone are, as remarked, far from common. Once alive to the value of metal and the possibility of transmuting stones into it, men must have sought deliberately for suitable ores and made numerous experiments, trying first one stone and then another. Many were fruitless, but other metals were discovered in the quest. Silver and lead both occur in prehistoric graves in Egypt, and were extensively used in Mesopotamia before 3000 B.C. Beads of meteoric iron occur in Egyptian graves shortly before 3000 B.C., and a little later iron ores were occasionally smelted in Mesopotamia. But on an industrial scale iron was not smelted nor worked anywhere before 1400 B.C. Tin was known to the metallurgists of Sumer and the Indus valley soon after 3000 B.C., being employed chiefly as an alloy of copper to simplify the process of casting.

The first copper ores to be exploited were presumably derived from surface deposits. Many such lodes must once have existed, but have been exhausted long before modern geological surveys were started. Eventually, however, men had to follow the vein beneath the ground and begin mining. The copper miner had to learn how to split hard rocks by kindling fires against them and throwing water on the heated surfaces. Systems of propping and timbering had to be devised to support the walls and roofs of the galleries. The ore had to be broken up, separated from the rock by washing, and transported to the surface. No records, however, survive to illustrate the steps by which the science of mining was founded; but by 1000 B.C. copper miners, even in still-barbarous Europe, were applying a science that a layman today can admire, but cannot attempt to expound.

The art of smelting is no less abstruse. As in casting, some sort of a blast is essential. And for production on a large scale a furnace had to be devised. And only surface ores of copper can be directly reduced by heating with charcoal; deeper ores are generally sulphides, and have to be roasted in the open to oxidize them before they can be smelted. Other metals require different treatment. Lead, for example, will volatilize and vanish with the smoke if its ore be heated in the sort of open furnace used for smelting copper.

Prospectors, miners, and smelters must therefore command a body of knowledge even more abstruse than that demanded of the smith. They must have classified the different kinds of ore, learned the outward signs for their diagnosis, the appropriate techniques for their treatment. The requisite knowledge could only be gained by experimentation and comparison of results on an even larger scale than was demanded by metalworking. Mining must have been an even more specialized trade than that of the smith. Miners as a rule cannot have been food-producers, but must have relied on a surplus of foodstuffs produced by those who consumed their products.

Intelligent metallurgy must have been widely understood in the Ancient East soon after 4000 B.C. But metal ousted stone very slowly. The advantages, stressed above, must not be exaggerated. For hoeing up the soil, stone blades serve the cultivator well; he will often have to replace them, but normally that is easy. A flint blade works excellently for cutting up carcasses, for reaping grains, for trimming leather, and even for shaving; it wears out quickly, but a new knife or razor can be fashioned in a few minutes where flint is abundant. Stone axes or adzes will fell trees, shape posts, or hew out a canoe almost as quickly and neatly as copper ones; only you will have to pause periodically and make a new axe from a convenient pebble. The chief defect of stone tools was that they wore out so quickly. But when the raw materials were lying about and time was not absurdly precious, it was not an intolerable hardship to have to make new tools from time to time. It needed the special geographical conditions of an alluvial plain, where suitable stones were rare, to drive home the value of the new and more permanent material and to create an effective and general demand for metal. And to make the satisfaction of that demand possible, improved methods of transport were needed. That meant the harnessing of animal motive power and of the winds. Both were, like the discovery of metal and the invention of metallurgy, preconditions of the second revolution and achieved before it.

Harnessing the strength of oxen or asses and the forces of the wind was man's first effective essay in making natural force work for him. When he had succeeded, he found himself for the first time controlling and even directing continuous forces not supplied by his own muscles. He was on the right road to releasing his body from the more brutal forms of physical labor—the road that leads to the internal-combustion engine and the electric motor, the steam hammer and the mechanical navvy. And at the same time he was learning new principles in mechanics and physics. . . .

It is easy enough to make guesses as to how the wheel might have been invented, but reliable data on the subject are hard to obtain. As wooden objects cannot normally last many centuries, the archaeologist can only learn about vehicles from people who happen to have left drawings or models of them in some durable material like pottery or stone. Their admittedly defective and one-sided testimony justifies the following positive statements: Wheeled vehicles are represented in Sumerian art as early as 3500 B.C., and in North Syria perhaps even earlier. By 3000 B.C. carts, wagons, and even chariots were in general use in Elam, Mesopotamia, and Syria. In the Indus valley wheeled carts were in use when the archaeological record begins about 2500 B.C., and at about the same date in Turkestan too. Some five centuries later, at least, they are attested in Crete and Asia Minor. On the other hand, the device was definitely not used by the Egyptians till about 1650 B.C., when it was forced upon them by Asiatic invaders, the Hyksos. . . .

The wheel not only revolutionized transport, it was already applied in manufacturing industry by 3500 B.C., and a brief digression is needed to explain this. With a horizontal wheel, at the center of which he can set his lump of clay spinning, the potter can shape in a couple of minutes a vessel that it would take several days to build up by hand. And the product will be more symmetrical. Pot-making was the first mechanized industry, the first to apply the wheel to manufacturing machinery. And the craft was transformed as a result. Ethnography shows that among the simpler people today the making of pots by hand is a domestic craft plied by the women, whereas manufacture on the wheel is a specialized trade reserved to men. The available evidence suggests that the same was true of antiquity. And so the introduction of the wheel into the ceramic industry marks another step in the specialization of labor; the potters are now specialists, withdrawn from the primary task of food-production and exchanging their wares for a share in the communal surplus. . . .

The introduction of wheeled vehicles drawn by oxen or other beasts accelerated communications and enormously simplified the transportation of goods. Vehicles do not, however, represent the sole method of employing animal motive power in transportation. Goods can be loaded directly on a beast's back and men can sit there. About 2000 B.C. merchandise was normally carried between Babylonia and Asia Minor on donkey-back. The history of this sort of transport is even harder to decipher in the archaeological record than is that of vehicular traffic. The donkey is native to Northeast Africa, and must have been domesticated there long before 3000 B.C., presumably to act as a beast of burden. Tame asses are recorded in Egypt by the date just mentioned, and at the same time were being employed to draw plows in Mesopotamia. Thereafter the ass remains the commonest beast of burden and riding-animal in the Near East. . . .

Parallel with the foregoing improvements in land transport went developments in navigation. But the evidence is even more scanty than just surveyed. Dugout canoes and skin-boats must have been used by fishers before the first revolution. Soon after it paintings on prehistoric Egyptian vases disclose substantial boats made of bundles of papyrus lashed together, propelled by forty or more rowers or paddlers, and equipped with a sort of cabin near the center. But sailboats are not depicted in Egypt till a little after 3500 B.C., and seem to belong to a type foreign to the Nile. Yet it is almost certain that by 3000 B.C. at latest sailboats were freely navigating the eastern Mediterranean. Though there is even less direct evidence, the same statement would surely apply to the Arabian Sea too.

Thus men have begun to overcome the mechanical difficulties in the way of marine transport (they have, that is, learned to build plank boats and to rig sails), and have acquired sufficient topographical and astronomical knowledge to utilize the highways of the sea. By water, as by land, the people of the Orient were now in position to pool their natural resources and the experience they were severally building up.

The arts, processes, and contrivances just enumerated are outward expressions of a body of science and applications of accumulated experience. Their diffusion means also the pooling of that practical knowledge. It equipped the peoples of the Orient with the technical control over Nature requisite for the completion of a second revolution, the establishment of a new type of economy and society. But other factors intervened before the knowledge thus acquired was applied in actual practice. . . .

It is believed that the "clash of cultures" set up by invasion and immigration facilitates the spread of new ideas by breaking down the rigidity of established societies. To survive, any society must attain an adjustment to its environment; it lives by exploiting the natural resources of its territory. But just insofar as the adjustment achieved is successful, the community concerned will tend to become conservative. When a group are enjoying a sufficiency of food in simple comfort with spells of rest, why should they change their behavior? They have painfully learned the tricks and dodges, the arts and crafts necessary to coax this modicum of prosperity out of Nature; why do more? Indeed, change may be dangerous. The success of simply equipped societies depends on everyone doing what has proved to be the right thing at the right time and in the proper way; it imposes a complete pattern of behavior on all the community's members. This pattern finds expression in social institutions and in traditional rules and prohibitions. It is sanctified by magico-religious beliefs and fears. Just as the practical acts of life are accompanied by appropriate rites and ceremonies, so mystical forces are supposed to watch over the traditional rules and avenge any transgression of them. The established economy is reinforced by an appropriate ideology.

The force of superstitions that consolidate and maintain established social institutions and economic arrangements is enormous in the simpler societies of today. It must have been so too in the

Ancient East. The adjustment then achieved by even the most favored communities was, after all, very precarious. An insufficient or an excessive flood, an untimely hailstorm, a plague of locusts, might imperil the whole community; for its resources were restricted, its reserves were small. But the disasters threatening its life are mysterious and even today incalculable. They might very easily be regarded as supernatural interventions, inflicted to avenge transgressions of customary rules of behavior. Any divergence from established practice, any departure from behavior that had been found safe and effective, might theoretically provoke such punishments. Any innovation was therefore dangerous, and public opinion would frown upon change. . . .

Now the first revolution had not abolished magic. Quite the reverse. Man, let us insist again, was still dependent on the incalculable chances of rain, flood, sunshine, still exposed to disaster from droughts, earthquakes, hailstorms, and other natural but unpredictable catastrophes. He still sought to control the beneficent forces and to ward off noxious powers by rituals, incantations, and charms. Anyone who could successfully claim to control the elements by his magic would, of course, earn immense prestige and authority. It is needless to demonstrate in detail how many opportunities of aggrandizement through alleged magical prowess must have presented themselves in ancient societies, but the chapter may be fitly closed with a reference to one great discovery: that of the solar calendar—that on one theory was one of the sources of royal authority in Egypt.

Farming in the Nile Valley is entirely dependent upon the annual flood; the latter's advent is the signal for the whole cycle of agricultural operations to start. To forecast precisely the day of its arrival and warn the peasant to prepare for it, would be and is of great advantage to all the valley's population. It would at the same time seem to be a proof of some sort of supernatural knowledge and power; the distinction between prediction and control is too subtle for simple peoples. Yet in reality the forecast can be made with considerable precision. The flood is a function of the annual movement of the earth round the sun—actually it depends upon the southwest monsoon breaking upon the mountains of Abyssinia. It will normally reach any given place at the same point in each of the earth's journeys round the sun—that is, on the same day in each solar year. All that is necessary, therefore, is to know the length of the solar year and reckon such a year from one observed flood as starting-point to the next.

Now most simple people who have any sort of calendar at all reckon by lunar months, and not by solar years, and there is evidence that the Egyptians were no exception to the rule. But no fixed number of lunar months (lunations) corresponds exactly to a solar year. To be able to predict the flood, therefore, the Egyptians had to determine the length of the solar year in days and devise an artificial calendar to reconcile solar and lunar years. Now observations recorded over a period of fifty years would suffice to show that the average interval between inundations was, to the nearest day, 365 days. On this basis an official calendar was introduced, most probably at the time of the unification of Egypt under Menes, in which the year of 365 days was divided into ten months of thirty-six days each, with a period of five intercalary days each year. It is difficult to see how even this result could have been obtained without written records, and it represents the first triumph of mathematical astronomy and the first vindication of the claim of science to predict. But of course there was an error in the calculation of just under six hours, and the accumulation of this error in time put the calendar entirely out of gear with the real seasons, and made it useless as a guide to the peasants in their agricultural work. New Year's Day originally coincided with the advent of the inundation, but after a century the inundation could not be expected until the 25th day of the first month. The royal officials discovered how to correct this error by observations on the star Sirius (Egyptian: Sothis) which, in the latitude of Cairo, is the last star to appear on the horizon before dawn obscures all stars at the flood season. They used their observations on the "heliacal rising" of Sirius to give the signal for the start of agricultural operations, but by this time it was too late to reform the official calendar—the requisite reform would have aroused the same sort of opposition, but naturally much more bitter, as has frustrated all attempts to fix the date of Easter. So the old official calendar was maintained, though the Egyptians recognized as Sothic cycles the periods of 1461 years when the official New Year's Day did actually coincide with the heliacal rising of Sirius.

Now historical kings in Egypt, as in Babylonia and elsewhere, were intimately connected with the regulation of the calendar. It has been suggested that they owed their authority in part at least to that first application of predictive service, the establishment of the calendar. The Pharaohs may even have kept secret the further discovery of the utility of the heliacal rising of Sirius as a sign of the flood's proximity to exploit it for their own prestige. The knowledge would have enabled the Pharaoh to predict the flood to the fellahin, and thus vindicate his magical powers of controlling the seasons and the crops. That is perhaps just a nice speculation. The determination of the solar year and the creation of an official calendar dependent on the standard are historical facts of the highest importance for the history of science. For the Egyptian is admittedly the parent of all Old World solar calendars, including our own. . . .

*   *   *

Almost from the outset of his career, it would seem, man used his distinctively human faculties not only to make substantial tools for use upon the real world, but also to imagine supernatural forces that he could employ upon it. He was, that is, simultaneously trying to understand, and so utilize, natural processes and peopling the real world with imaginary beings, conceived in his own image, that he hoped to coerce or cajole. He was building up science and superstition side by side.

The superstitions man devised and the fictitious entities he imagined were presumably necessary to make him feel at home in his environment and to make life bearable. Nevertheless the pursuit of the vain hopes and illusory shortcuts suggested by magic and religion repeatedly deterred man from the harder road to the control of Nature by understanding. Magic seemed easier than science, just as torture is less trouble than the collection of evidence.

Magic and religion constituted the scaffolding needed to support the rising structure of social organization and of science. Unhappily the scaffolding repeatedly cramped the execution of the design and impeded the progress of the permanent building. It even served to support a sham facade behind which the substantial structure was threatened with decay. The urban revolution, made possible by science, was exploited by superstition. The principal beneficiaries from the achievements of farmers and artisans were priests and kings. Magic rather than science was thereby enthroned and invested with the authority of temporal power.

It is as futile to deplore the superstitions of the past as it is to complain of the unsightly scaffolding essential to the erection of a lovely building. It is childish to ask why man did not progress straight from the squalor of a "pre-class" society to the glories of a classless paradise, nowhere fully realized as yet. Perhaps the conflicts and contradictions, above revealed, themselves constitute the dialectics of progress. In any case, they are facts of history. If we dislike them, that does not mean that progress is a delusion, but merely that we have understood neither the facts nor progress nor man. Man made the superstitions and the institutions of oppression as much as he made the sciences and the instruments of production. In both alike he was expressing himself, finding himself, making himself.

Grahame Clark
NATURAL SELECTION AND THE ADVENT OF CIVILIZATION

Some authorities have argued that Childe's account of the advent of civilization is unacceptable due to the unscientific nature of his methodology. One of the most trenchant critics of the "Childe thesis" is Grahame Clark, a leading exponent of Darwin's theory of evolution. Clark maintains that man, his environment, and everything in it are the products of natural selection, and that it is the gravest of errors to suggest that "man has made himself." Clark has served at Cambridge University as university lecturer, head of the Department of Archaeology and Anthropology, and as the Disney Professor of Archaeology. His publication career spans over three decades and he has lectured at many of the leading academic institutions around the world.

When prehistorians consider the archaeological evidence for man's emergence as a new kind of animal, they are bound, if they are concerned with its meaning, to ask themselves how it was that in the course of a few tens of thousands of generations a new and specifically human way of life appeared in our universe. Why are we not still a grimacing bunch of nonhuman primates? How and why have the

From Grahame Clark, *Aspects of Prehistory* (Berkeley, 1970). Originally published by the University of California Press; reprinted by permission of the Regents of the University of California. Footnotes omitted.

manifold changes that comprised man's prehistory come about? Why have they proceeded at an ever accelerating pace? Why are we still not bashing out pebble tools or even hand axes? How did we come to eat bread? What do the material advances in technology, land occupation, and subsistence portend, and how do we explain them?

Men have, ever since they began to be aware of their context in time, been concerned with how they came to be what they are. Among preliterate peoples the prevailing material culture, social institutions, and even physical environment are commonly accepted as the work of ancestors or culture heroes. As men became literate the origins of all such things came to be ascribed to the creative, innovating achievements of gods and their particular servants, achievements embodied in scriptures or sacred writings. More recently, explanations have returned to the anthropomorphic level, but this time it has no longer been mythological or legendary heroes but unknown artificers or food winners who have been held to have shaped human destiny. Only a generation ago, Gordon Childe entitled a still famous book *Man Makes Himself* and Arnold Toynbee in his *Study of History* constantly returned to the theme of men responding or failing to respond to challenges. It is, indeed, ironical that the image of man entertained by some humanists as the creator of his own destiny has been fed by an exaggerated notion of the role of natural scientists whose achievement has been in reality no more revolutionary than the winning of a partial insight into natural processes. So far as anthropology is concerned, it may be doubted whether an anthropomorphic explanation of prehistory has much to tell us. Indeed, one is compelled to ask whether attempts to dramatize the past in such terms do not interfere with our proper task. Is it really sensible or profitable to think of man as something apart from the world in which he has his being? Are we not really concerned with a process, the process that has not merely shaped men and their cultures, but all other forms of life and indeed our universe and all the other universes of which we are becoming increasingly aware?

It is plain that if we accept the full implications of *The Origin of Species,* if we acknowledge without reserve that man and his works are in truth a product of the same evolutionary forces as have shaped the universe, then we can hardly view him as making himself or challenging nature. The contrary has of course to be faced that, if man really made himself, then it would be a waste of time to consider prehistory in any other light than as an almost hopelessly defective kind of history. To a historian with full documentary and biographical sources it is possible to treat history as a kind of morality play: the characters appear briefly on the stage, interact with others, make their choices, and submit to the judgment of the historian. In such a play particularity of persons and circumstances is everything; but it is precisely this which is by definition beyond the reach of the prehistorian. The wise student of man's past must observe a certain tact if he is not to waste his time; above all he should confine himself to problems capable of being solved by the kind of evidence likely to be available. In studying the prehistoric past it is often futile or at least highly uneconomic to ask the kind of question that most keenly engages social anthropologists or the historians of literate societies. A sound argument for studying prehistory in the context of anthropology is surely that it facilitates a rational allocation of research goals. A main contribution that prehistorians can make to the general understanding is to investigate the operation over much longer periods of time than are available to social anthropologists or even to historians of the processes involved in the evolution of human society.

The thesis I would seek to propound is quite simply that man and his way of life as this has developed down to the present day are both ultimately the product of natural selection. In saying this one has, of course, to make many reservations. It hardly needs emphasizing that, whereas biological evolution has proceeded on a genetic basis, cultural evolution rests on a social basis. Culture is shared and transmitted by virtue of belonging to particular communities that are in themselves constituted by sharing particular traditions. Natural selection could nevertheless operate on cultural variations as well as on genetic mutations. As we shall see (p. 117), cultural diversity was by no means the only source of variability in human society; the emergence and enrichment of human personality was another potent source of deviation on which the forces of natural selection could play. A fact of the utmost significance insofar as social evolution is concerned is that the powers of articulate speech and in the long run of writing and electronics, by facilitating the storing and accumulation of information, have caused cultural evolution in the world at large to accelerate at an ever-increasing pace.

It is fortunate that the aspect of human behavior which has left its clearest imprint on the archaeological record is that concerned with technology and subsistence, since it is precisely in the context of economic life that natural selection has operated most clearly and demonstrably. The records of economic life are as much there for study as are the bones of extinct animals. Prehistorians are indeed cultural paleontologists. The artifacts on which prehistoric archaeologists have to work are veritable fossils of human life. Tools, after all, were used to manipulate and shape the environment; clothes and their fastenings, not to mention houses, to provide shelter; weapons to hunt wild animals and contend with other men in the spacing out of territory; digging sticks, spades, and plows for cultivating the ground; and skis, sledges, wheeled vehicles, and boats for traversing land and water. The use of these and the many other categories of material equipment is not in doubt. In Childe's vivid analogy man's implements and indeed his whole material equipment can be regarded as extracorporeal limbs. They serve his purposes as an organism. The fact that men shaped their flints and stones in accordance with socially inherited traditions, whereas lions and tigers owe their teeth and claws to genetic inheritance, does not alter the fact that the biological effectiveness of artifacts as of physical attributes is determined by their fitness for the task in hand. In relation to human society, natural selection has operated through the economic arrangements by which men have sought to extract a living from the world in which they live. . . .

It follows from what has been said earlier . . . about the nature of human culture that it can hardly have developed along a course of unilinear evolution. Social evolution was polycentric, developing in many distinct though interconnected areas. The immense range of environments occupied by man would alone ensure that natural selection would result in a variety of cultural manifestations at any one moment of time. But this is not the only reason why we do not see mankind everywhere developing along uniform lines; one has to remember that every advance in the complexity of social life opened up an increasingly large number of alternatives. The existence of distinct cultural manifestations in neighboring territories—and at an advanced stage of social evolution at different levels in the same communities—was of extreme importance from an evolutionary point of view, because it offered a wide range of alternatives on which the process of selection could play. Although economic competition was never perfect between human societies, it nevertheless existed and in the long term it provided the most important medium through which selection could operate. In practice this competition between alternative answers to analogous problems occurred much more often in the context of peaceful acculturation than in that of conflict. Indeed, it might be said that up to a point frequency and intensity of culture contact was a controlling factor in cultural development; for no significant human societies have ever existed permanently in complete isolation, and those most cut off from contacts were as a rule those most marginal to centers of rapid advance.

This and the fact that the main drift of evolution in the sphere of economics has been in the same direction, that is toward obtaining the maximum return for the minimum expenditure of effort, means that behind the diversity of cultural expression it should in fact be possible to discern underlying regularities. In the context of world history it is for some purposes the regularities rather than the idiosyncracies that are most directly relevant. In the realm of the lithic industries that provide the skeletal framework of the technology for all but the last two hundred and fifty generations of men, it is useful for some purposes to distinguish a series of modes. The idea that the basic modus operandi of prehistoric industries has undergone a broad development in time is one that has been entertained by distinguished archaeologists in the past in relation to both lithic and metallurgical technology. In relation to flint and stone working, the evidence is now clearer and full enough to justify further consideration.

In reviewing the succession of modes that transcended cultural idioms in lithic production, one must bear in mind certain qualifications. First it is hardly to be expected that lithic industries should necessarily be sharply defined from one another. Techniques that, when applied on a broad front, helped to define a new mode might be and in fact normally were present or latent in earlier ones, only coming forward as dominant traits when selected to fill a newly emerged need; and on the other hand methods dominant in one mode were frequently combined with those of later ones, resulting in industries that might be classified as hybrids of two or even more modes. Yet the fact that the lithic industries made and used by particular communities rarely conform narrowly to any one mode does not invalidate the concept for certain kinds of discourse. The second main qualification to be borne in mind is that not all our modes were of universal occurrence. Indeed, we know that none were, even if certain techniques were, so to speak, incorporated in the general heritage of mankind. We have to remember that in the course of prehistory the habitat of man underwent a great expansion so that the first modes were practiced in their pristine manner only in the cortical zone of the hominids. Conversely, it may well be that modes 3 and 4 emerged as a result of natural selection in the more northerly territories occupied during the Upper Pleistocene.[1]

Mode 1. . . . The earliest method of working flint or stone tools was extremely elementary. The stoneworker merely hammered off a few flakes from a pebble or other nodule. In this way he might produce flake tools that might be used even without further retouch and heavier forms that could have been used for chopping, cutting, or scraping. Industries in this mode occur in Lower or early Middle Pleistocene deposits over the warmer parts of the Old World from Africa and Europe to Southwest Asia and North China, to which human settlement appears to have been confined at this time.

Mode 2. A new mode was established during the Middle Pleistocene when flint and stone knappers extended secondary flaking over both faces of the residual tool. Quite plainly this mode stemmed from the preceding one and presumably arose because it provided more effective tools that would for this reason have been selected for survival in the normal course of evolution. Where a succession of industries can be established, as in parts of North Africa and in the Rift Valley of East Africa, it is possible to observe the appearance first of the bifacial flaking technique and then of the extension of this over the whole or the greater part of both faces of the nodule in such a way as to expand the effective perimeter.

Industries characterized above all by bifacial hand axes were concentrated in southern Europe and Africa with parts of Southwest Asia and peninsular India. Within this tradition there is evidence in some areas for progressive refinement in technique during the course of

[1] Pleistocene refers to the Ice Age, which began about two million years ago and ended approximately 10,000 B.C. The Pleistocene must be regarded as central to the evolution of human technology and society. It created environmental challenges and opportunities that stimulated the movement of peoples to new environments, and prompted the invention of appropriate tools and forms of social organization to cope with the new environment.—Ed.

time, and there was obviously scope for wide variation in relation to local ecological circumstances. Bifacial techniques failed to spread as far east as China and Southeast Asia; in these territories industries continued to be made in mode 1 and it was these that were first carried to Australia.

Mode 3. At a fairly early stage of the Upper Pleistocene, a new mode developed in an area overlapping the northern part of the hand-ax zone in North Africa, Europe, and parts of Southwest Asia and extending into the newly settled territories of South Russia as far east as Uzbekistan. The emphasis lay on the production of flakes from carefully prepared cores. In some industries these were shaped like a tortoise so that a flake could be struck from the convex face in a form ready for immediate use, though for particular purposes these might be trimmed on one or two edges to make "points" or "scrapers"; in others, cores might be of simpler disc form; and in either case industries might or might not be accompanied by hand axes carried forward from mode 2. In the course of time mode 3 techniques penetrated almost the whole of the former hand-ax territory of Africa, in parts of which they, indeed, became dominant. Again, there is evidence for a marked trend toward the use of flake tools struck from prepared cores in peninsular India.

Mode 4. A significant change occurred with the appearance between thirty and forty thousand years ago of industries based on the production of regular blades struck by a punch technique from carefully prepared elongated cores. These formed blanks from which a much greater variety of objects could be shaped, including knives, end scrapers, projectile points, and gravers or burins. These last may well have been developed mainly for cutting up and shaping animal bone, antler, and ivory, of which much more sophisticated use was made by practitioners of mode 4 industries; and, again, for engraving representations on antler and bone artifacts and on rock surfaces in executing the art recovered from an extensive territory from Iberia to Siberia. The new mode apparently developed within the territory of the preceding one, but it was evidently carried by pioneers over extensive territories to the north and east. In European Russia, settlement extended to 55 degrees north; and east of the Urals, bearers of a mode 4 technology, pressed into Japan, northeastern Siberia and the New World. In many industries of this mode use continued to be made of the bifacial technique of mode 2 for such special purposes as projectile points; and in some, these points were the most immediately prominent features. Other mode 4 industries, for instance in Siberia, were enriched by techniques proper to mode 3.

Mode 5. Certain industries of mode 4 included an element of small, often minute, flints (microliths) shaped by the same blunting technique as some larger forms. At the close of the Ice Age and during the Neothermal period this element, and the various forms of slotted haft for which they were designed, became so prominent that one may justly speak of a distinctive mode. Industries in mode 5 are of particular interest because they were dominant in the Old World during the period of transition from economies based on hunting and gathering to those depending at least to some degree on farming. The device of composite weapons with inset microliths was widely adopted over Southwest Asia, Europe, extensive tracts of Africa, and southern and eastern Asia, whence they spread on the one hand to Australia and on the other to the Arctic territories of Alaska, northern Canada, and Greenland.

Mode 6. The last significant and widespread mode of working flint and stone was marked by highly polished axes or adzes, which first became of crucial importance in habitats supporting a climax vegetation of forest trees. Experiments have shown that polished flint axes were able to fell trees with less effort than ones with chipped edges. Thus, under circumstances in which tree-felling was important, polished blades would be favored by natural selection over merely chipped ones. This applied with special force where farming was carried on in a forested landscape, since woodland had to be cleared for cultivation and the creation of pasture. It is hardly surprising to find polished stone blades playing an important role in the peasant societies of southwest and southern Asia, as well as in the Far East; in Mediterranean and temperate Europe; over much of Africa; in Mesoamerica and parts of temperate North America; in New Guinea and Melanesia; and not least in Polynesia, where they were additionally important for shaping the canoes without which the islands could hardly have been occupied. But the use of polished stone blades was by no means confined to societies based on farming; it was, for instance, a basic component of the culture of the hunter-fishers of the circumpolar zone of the northern hemisphere. . . .

The advances in technology incorporating new methods of production and the utilization of a wider range of raw materials made it possible for *Homo sapiens* to expand his range of settlement and occupy a wider range of environments. As we have noted, *Homo erectus,* who depended on industries in modes 1 and 2, was mainly confined to the relatively warm territories long occupied by non-human primates, even though he had already, early in the Middle Pleistocene, occupied lands sufficiently far north to place a selective advantage on the use and production of fire. Some further northward expansion was achieved by *Homo sapiens neanderthalensis,* who disposed of mode 3 industries that included specialized scraping equipment of a kind well adapted to the preparation of animal skins for clothing and shelter. A dramatic expansion, involving broad tracts of northern Eurasia and extending into the New World, was left to modern man. (*Homo sapiens sapiens*) who in his northern territories disposed in the closing stages of the Upper Pleistocene of the more advanced industries made possible by the adoption of mode 4 techniques. Finally, it was the adoption of mode 6, making it comparatively easy to shape the timbers of sea-going boats, that made it possible for man to traverse even extensive tracts of the Pacific Ocean and occupy islands over its surface.

Broad changes can likewise be seen in the realm of subsistence. The first change and one that in a sense symbolized the appearance of man was the shift from an almost exclusively vegetarian diet to one in which animal protein came to play a role of substantial importance. Like all attempts at historical reconstruction and like much of the rest of human knowledge, this change is still hypothetical; the existing great apes are certainly not the first ancestors of man, and the diet of these ancestors is still unknown. Nevertheless, it is at least suggestive that the great apes, though basically dependent on plant food, relish animal protein when it comes their way, which suggests that they were vegetarian more by circumstance than by choice. Thanks to the researches of Dr. and Mrs. Leakey[2] at Olduvai, it appears that already during the Lower Pleistocene certain forms of Australopithacine *(A. africanus,* cf. *Homo habilis)* were supplementing their predominantly vegetarian diet by small animals like lizards,

[2] Dr. and Mrs. L. S. B. Leakey were a famous British husband-and-wife team of anthropologists, who in 1964 discovered at Olduvai Gorge in Tanzania what they claimed was the earliest representative of the genus *Homo.*—Ed.

rodents, and birds, as well as by scavenging big game. It was the shaping of effective weapons, notably wooden spears, that first made it possible for certain primates to hunt animals, in some cases more powerful than themselves, and the ability to do so effectively marked them as men. In terms of economic activity the change of diet implied a shift from a monotonous routine of foraging to one in which this basic activity was complemented by hunting. Socially this was of the utmost significance because, whereas the routine of foraging was shared equally by both sexes and by individuals of all ages, the addition of hunting led to increased differentiation in the roles of male and female in the food quest: hunting was an activity to which man, the more active partner in sexual relationships and physically more powerful because selected for this role of dominance, was by his very nature better adapted. The hunting of big game did far more than underline and deepen the economic partnership of the sexes, a basis of the institution of the human family; by necessitating the co-operation of several males it promoted the development of social groupings comprising a number of family units.

The key importance of hunting became even more manifest after early man had penetrated territories lying to the north of what might be termed the homeland of the primates. A crucial pioneering role was played by the peoples who first occupied the northern marches of the Paleolithic world and whose principal memorials are lithic industries in mode 3, but it was not until between thirty and forty thousand years ago that we find clear evidence among the makers of mode 4 industries of a pronounced intensification in the activity of hunting. This took the form both of a more highly differentiated weaponry . . . and of a graphic art which, whatever else is said about it, bears witness to an intense observation of and identification with wild animals. Some of the most splendid memorials of the advanced hunters of the Late Glacial period in parts of western Europe were the representations of game animals on the walls and ceilings of caves like Altamira and Lascaux.

A further change and one that underlay and made possible the development of the various literate civilizations of man was the adoption of farming. The crucial significance of what Gordon Childe once termed the "Neolithic Revolution" is amply documented in the archaeological record. No society dependent on catching or gathering has ever achieved literate civilization on its own; and, conversely, all literate civilizations can be seen to have developed from and still to depend ultimately upon the practice of farming. This fact is undisputed, and Childe more than any other scholar established it as part of conventional wisdom. . . .

Historically speaking, Childe's thesis stemmed from the contrast drawn by Sir John Lubbock in his *Prehistoric Times* (1865) between Paleolithic hunter-gatherers and Neolithic farmers, groups held at that time to have been sundered by a temporal hiatus in Europe, the only part of the world whose prehistory had then been even partly explored. The continuity of prehistory has only been restored by more intensive work in Europe and above all by the extension of systematic exploration to the Near East. Nor has this been done merely in a temporal sense. The dichotomy between hunting and gathering on the one hand and stock-raising and agriculture on the other is no longer so clearly defined as it was by Lubbock or Childe. The notion that food gatherers were only capable of grubbing or snatching whatever wild plant food was going was a stereotype of the way in which civilized men once regarded those he thought of as primitive. The situation reported by modern field anthropologists is very different. We know that in reality plant gatherers, like many hunters, required a detailed knowledge of the habits and characteristics of a much greater variety of species than modern farmers. An inhabitant of Cape York Peninsula or of the arid interior of Australia gathers not one or two harvests, but a plentitude in accordance with a pattern far more intricate than that of our farmers' year. One difference between fully committed farmers and gatherers, in fact, is precisely that the former in the long run restrict themselves to a much narrower range of plants, those they have sown themselves. But this change was not a sudden or clear-cut one. . . .

It was not until the forces of selection operating through subsistence economics made it more profitable to concentrate on sown plants that wild ones ceased to be important for food; and even when this had happened they continued, as we know from the recent peasant cultures of Europe, to be gathered for a great variety of purposes, aromatic, industrial, magical, and medicinal. The determining factor was presumably the adoption of a fully sedentary habit which placed a premium on plants sown close at hand as against those gathered from an extensive range of countryside. . . .

Again, if we turn to the question of sowing as opposed to gathering, we find no clear-cut difference. There is no suggestion that planting the first crop was the result of a bright idea by some deserving pioneer of the human race. Indeed, the distinction between self-propagating and intentionally sown is not merely difficult, but indeed impossible for us to distinguish at this distance in time; it may be doubted whether it was known to prehistoric man himself. The change is surely one to be explained more convincingly in terms of the evolutionary process. If wild plants were brought home, as they must have been to be consumed, they would surely have sown themselves. It is not difficult to imagine that the surroundings of the homestead enriched by domestic refuse, not to mention the dung of livestock, would have provided conditions far more favorable for growth than those occurring in their natural habitats. And this factor would naturally have assumed added importance as settlement became more permanent; for the richer the accumulation of phosphates and nitrogen, the more rewarding the returns of sown crops, which would for this very reason enjoy an adaptive advantage over wild ones. . . .

One could continue in this vein, but enough has been said to make the point that the technology and subsistence of early man was shaped by natural selection operating on cultures adapted to all the various environments in which he lived. Again, it is worth re-emphasizing that this process could only operate effectively when confronted by variables. It is emphatically not the case that men everywhere and under all circumstances utilized their environment to the limit of their technology. So long as we realize that *Homo economicus* is a lay figure who never, in fact, walked the earth, there is no harm in using him as a model, if only to point up the noneconomic motivations of human behavior. In reality societies, insofar as they are human, harbor values that are inherited from the past, often from a remote past when quite different forms of economic and social life prevailed. Human beings are prepared to pay a price in terms of economic efficiency to maintain sacred cows of one kind or another. Yet even irrational behavior, provided it motivates people sufficiently strongly, may in fact have an adaptive value by increasing productivity. Again, ideological, traditional, and other noneconomic patterns of behavior may be important in another way, simply by increasing the range of variability on which natural selection could play.

In the long run—and prehistorians have to think in terms of long periods of time if they are to make their special contribution to anthropological discourse—it is still true that natural selection operates in favor of those most capable of understanding and exploiting their environment. It is suggestive in this connection that W. W. Rostrow in his key paper on "The Take-off into Self-Contained Growth" has characterized economic growth as being in "the essentially biological field." One is entitled to think that he had it in mind to do more than merely point out the analogy between economic and biological growth; he meant, surely, that economic growth was of the same essential character as biological growth, in the sense that both enlarged the possibilities of life and were subject to the same fundamental process of natural selection and evolution. Basically the cultures of which prehistoric archaeologists study the material traces served in their time as mechanisms by means of which communities of men sustained not merely life, but the good life, the life that enshrined values and called forth the greatest effort to realize them. The fact that the production of artifacts was subject to the evolutionary process has obvious implications for the methodology of archaeology. In particular it highlights the need to focus attention on progressive changes in basic processes such as working flint, potting, or metallurgy. From this point of view it is fortunate that modern technology has itself necessitated the development of the conceptual tools and hardware needed for rapid statistical analysis. Imperfect though competition between communities may have been, it seems evident that those people flourished most, and therefore left the main impression on the archaeological record, that were most efficient not merely at a technical level but in terms of social achievement. Natural selection must always and necessarily have favored those who showed themselves most adaptable to circumstances as these arose and most capable of exerting themselves effectively.

I have spoken of communities and of the processes which shaped the course of their history over long periods of time. What of the individuals who compose societies? Do not human societies differ from animal societies in that they consist of beings capable of thought and of exercising choice? Is one guilty of crass determinism in suggesting that men are subject to the same processes of change that have called into shape not merely the world in which we live, but all those universes that human ingenuity is now allowing us to apprehend?

At this time of day there is surely no need to debate the problem of free will; the statistical models we devise to gain a more precise understanding of the physical world, let alone of social behavior, take due account of the factors of randomness and deviance. An individual man or for that matter an individual mosquito enjoys at any particular moment a freedom of choice limited only by organic attributes and the constraints of the environment. In relation to evolution, on the other hand, the behavior of individuals is only relevant insofar as it affects the species or the community.

By and large and under most circumstances, the deviations of individuals have been ineffective in the sense that they have normally failed to deflect or modify social behavior. Yet it is certain that personal dissent has been critically important for the evolution of culture; it provided precisely the variant on which natural selection could operate at some critical juncture in social history, very much as mutations served in the field of biological evolution. When one technique replaced another or when forms were modified, it was not due to some individual innovator so much as to the evolutionary process selecting the individual deviation that happened at some particular juncture to meet the needs of the situation most adequately. In this way, individual departures from the norm might be selected for survival and incorporated into the ongoing and changing pattern of group behavior.

It is a striking fact that taking the world as a whole, or more accurately the leading centers of innovation, the rate of cultural advance has undergone a marked and progressive acceleration in the course of time. For the earlier ages of mankind, change was so slow that its course could be measured in geological time and could only be detected in the short term by painstaking metrical and statistical analysis. At the same time the earliest industries of man (modes 1 and 2) were remarkable for their homogeneity over vast tracts of territory. It was not until an advanced stage of the Pleistocene that we find evidence for marked local variation and for more rapid change. It is surely no accident that this acceleration and this diversification should have occurred at precisely the same time as convincing evidence arises for self-awareness and by implication for a marked growth in individual thought and feeling. The forces of natural selection had progressively more variables on which to play as cultural traditions grew more complex and diverse and as individuals grew in self-awareness and capacity for thought. The attainment of a settled way of life, based on farming, was another factor to accelerate the pace of change. For one thing the mere fact of being tied to particular localities in itself made for greater regional differences in cultural style. Secondly, as Gordon Childe emphasized, the opportunity that farming gave for people to live and work together in larger communities made it possible for craftsmen to engage in a much greater degree of specialization, which in itself led to a large number of ways of solving particular problems or in other words to a greater range of choice and, therefore, of variability. Although the civilizations that developed from the formative stage of settled life shared certain basic features as a class, it is characteristic of them that wherever they developed they display idiosyncracies of style and sometimes of form. This is nowhere more clearly displayed than in the scripts . . . in which their earliest written records were inscribed. The development of writing—like that of metallurgy, agriculture, lithic technology, and indeed almost any manifestation of culture one can think of—developed along idosyncratic lines in many different centers. This was eloquently expressed by Henri Frankfort in his comparison of the two earliest literate civilizations of the Old World: "A comparison between Egypt and Mesopotamia discloses, not only that writing, representational art, monumental architecture, and a new kind of political coherence was introduced in the two countries; it also reveals that the purpose of their writing, the contents of their representations, the functions of their monumental buildings, and the structure of their new societies differed completely. What we observe is not merely the establishment of civilized life, but the emergence, concretely, of the distinctive 'forms' of Egyptian and Mesopotamian civilization." If the range of comparison is widened to comprehend, for example, the Indian, Chinese, Greek, and Mayan civilizations, all these points and many others can be made with even greater force.

Enough has probably been said to make the point that in the development of modes of subsistence, as of technology, there is no need to envisage culture heroes or revolutions; nor, *pace* Gordon Childe, is it appropriate to think in terms of drama. Instead we are confronted by the same processes as have fashioned ourselves and the universe as a whole; it is merely that they have operated in a different manner. If natural selection functioned in the case of animals through the gene pool, among men it has worked through the medium of culture, most obviously through technology and subsistence patterns, but also through social organization and value systems. The emergence during modern times of societies in which increasing resources are directed to the systematic investigation of natural processes has not altered the situation in any fundamental way; it is merely that the process of change has speeded up because the process of natural selection, which operates today to an important degree through state power, has more alternatives from which to choose. Cultural evolution proceeds apace. How or why it started and where it is heading are questions as difficult to answer as how or why it is that our universe began and where it is going. At least we can frame such questions even if we have to admit that we do not know the answers; and framing questions betrays a degree of self-awareness shared by no other animal.

Robert Redfield

THE CONCEPT OF REFORM AND THE ADVENT OF CIVILIZATION

Redfield maintains that the "making of man" with which Childe is concerned is little more than the unpremeditated development of tools and institutions. He would like to raise the question as to whether or not in the transformation of folk society to civilization, man can be seen as the conscious shaper of his own destiny? Redfield pursues his objective by tracing the development of the idea of reform and he demonstrates how this idea has been consciously used to alter human existence. However, in his final analysis he concludes that the idea of reform is a modern conception and, thus, primitive man can in no way be viewed as a conscious reformer. Originally a lawyer, Robert Redfield turned to anthropology in his early twenties and eventually became a recognized authority on Middle American folk culture. His outstanding contributions to both anthropology and education were recognized in 1953 when he became the Robert Maynard Hutchins Distinguished Service Professor, the highest scholastic position in the University of Chicago.

The title of this chapter ["Man Makes Himself"] is taken—as is much of the stimulation for this little book—from V. Gordon Childe. But the quotation marks around the phrase are also a sign that it is here put to a different use, pushed to a different meaning. In his book with this title Childe writes of the long historical development of tools and institutions wherein man, once a being not yet human, came to be the creature that he is now. The "making of man" with which Childe is concerned is unplanned. It is that making of man in which a future is made that men do not foresee or strive to bring about. The consequences of agriculture and of the building of cities were not intended. They just happened. The institutions in which civilization was founded were, in Sumner's terms, crescive, not enacted. In the early and very much longer part of his history man did not see himself as maker of either his future world or of himself. It is Childe, looking backward upon what happened in history, who sees man as the maker of himself.

On the other hand, in modern civilization as it appears both in the West and in the East, men commonly undertake to make their future world different from the one in which they live. The West invented progress and reform. The East today is in revolt; there is a great purpose to change things. The intentional making over of society is a conception of civilized man, perhaps only of modern man. May we not say that there was no Utopia prior to *The Republic?* But there have been many since, and most of these since the Renaissance. It is true that before Plato the Hebrew prophets looked forward to the building of the Kingdom of God on earth by those few who should be saved from the doom of nations. But the vision of Isaiah, like the visions of Wodziwob, the Paiute Indian prophet of the Second Ghost Dance, and of the prophets of the Vailala Madness of New Guinea, is a dream, a faith, not a plan. Such visions arose out of protests against the consequences of civilization or against the corruption of the traditional folk life. They are, in their nature and function, a link between the myths of primitive peoples and the positive plans of reform of modern peoples. In the throes of moral suffering people create an image of their hopes and fears. But it is at first a mere picture of those hopes and fears. Only later, with the further development of civilization, does the prospective myth become a Utopia and then a plan for action.

Man makes himself, then, in two senses, and the two senses imply a contrast between folk society and, at least, modern civilization. Man is self-made through the slow and unpremeditated growth of culture and civilization. Man later attempts to take control of this process and to direct it where he wills. The contrast suggests a topic and a problem. The topic is the transformation of the folk society into civilization through the appearance and development of the idea of reform, of alteration of human existence, including the alteration of man himself, by deliberate intention and design. The problem is the recognition of the roots of this conception—if any there be—in the primitive societies. It is only the first paragraphs of the story of this revolution in man's condition with which I dare concern myself, with that very little part of it which asks whether in societies primitive or precivilized man is in any significant degree the conscious shaper of his world.

"Reform," "planning," "constitutional amendment" are not categories that we are likely to find employed by an ethnologist reporting the way of life of a primitive society unaffected by civilization. Characteristically he will give us descriptions of customs and institutions, not accounts of people criticizing these customs and institutions, still less trying to create new ones. This may be the case because criticism and creation are not frequent and conspicuous in isolated primitive societies. It may also be because the training of the ethnologist is to record what is usual and institutional, not what is unusual and creatively novel. Where we do find something in an ethnologist's account that seems to represent the primitive people as critical of their own traditions or as reflecting systematically upon them, we may hesitate before accepting it as proof that the primitive people did think critically or philosophically uninfluenced by some representative of modern civilization. Moreover, the ethnologist himself is an influence on the native, and a further influence on the written form given to what the native tells him. In the very attempt to get information he stimulates in his informants a certain amount of reflection and even criticism. And in writing his ethnographic account, the ethnologist tends to put things into an arrangement that is convenient and perhaps esthetically attractive but that may suggest that the average native has a more systematic and reflective view of things than is actually true. All these circumstances reduce to a very small amount the dependable knowledge we have as to the reflective thought and creative action of primitive peoples in their aboriginal conditions.

Let us look first at the evidences for reflective thought in primitive societies. The evidence on which Paul Radin relies in his book *Primitive Man as Philosopher* is subject to the doubt I have mentioned. The Winnebago, and many of the other peoples from whom, directly or indirectly, Radin obtained the texts that indicate skeptical and systematic thinking, were affected by civilization when they told Radin or other students what they doubted or philosophized about. And the texts which Radin puts forward to show primitive skepticism were, in many cases, collected by missionaries. One wonders, for instance, if Bishop Callaway's own presence and activities affected the Amazulu natives who told him that though they thought about Unkulunkulu, their supreme deity, they were aware that none among them really knew about him; they told the Bishop also that they did things that were evil yet justified the doing "since it was made by Unkulunkulu." Few of the materials offered by Radin are perfect proof against the charge that it is a native mind set in motion by a civilized mind that is recorded.

Nevertheless, I think that we must accept the principal conclusion of Radin's book, that in primitive and precivilized societies there is some reflective, critical, and creative thinking. In the twenty-five years since the book appeared, I have seen no important refutation of it and have met a good deal that tends to confirm it. . . .

The evidence which Radin offers to show that in any primitive society there are some people who make explicit systems out of looser traditional ideas he finds principally in the high degree of systematic arrangement of abstract ideas in the origin myths and cosmological accounts of some primitive peoples. Here, it is the very elaboration of the way in which ideas are related to one another that is the evidence for the existence of the primitive philosopher; one does not actually see him philosophizing; he is inferred from what is taken to be his philosophy. Dr. James Walker reported the conceptions of the Oglala Sioux as to the circle as the basic pattern of the universe and the fundamental symbol of space and time. To this archetypal idea the Indian informant related sun, earth, the year, day, night, the tipi, and the camp circle. Accounts closely corresponding to this, similarly systematizing the universe and many things about man and his acts, I have obtained from Maya Indians of Yucatan; in their case it is the quadrilateral which is the basic and universal pattern. To read Walker's account of the circular universe as described by the Sioux . . . is to be persuaded that in at least some primitive societies a few people do think about the more general and popular ideas as to the nature of man and the universe and do give these ideas a new depth and consistency. . . .

To the evidence of such materials, I add my impression that most ethnologists who have worked intimately with isolated, nonliterate people who enjoy even a little time in which one might reflect find in such communities a few people who do reflect. The difference between one native, who acts without much thought, and the occasional native of a reflective and even speculative turn of mind, is apparent to one who has come to know a good many of the adults of a primitive community. Whether or not the intellectual refining of a more general and popular tradition by certain persons who have the time and the inclination to do so is to be called "speculation for its own sake," as Radin calls it, the main point that he makes appears to stick. In primitive as in civilized societies some people live unreflective and matter-of-fact lives, while a few others are disposed to speculation; and these latter accomplish some critical and even creative thought on problems of existence and conduct.

I see no reason to deny the probability that this much creative thinking took place before the first cities were built among some food producers, and even among some food-collecting "savages." The presence of some leisure seems a necessary condition for the first philosophy; we do not find systematic and critical thinking reported from the ever-hungry, frequently tired and sick Bolivian Siriono. The development of a priesthood with a specialized tradition is obviously another favorable precondition. But there seems to be no necessity that the appearance of such thinking had to await full-time specialists. . . .

Yet the specialized priests of the civilizations certainly greatly advanced such thinking. Systematization and skepticism—these two fruits of the speculative mind are to be found in many a study of the history of thought in the ancient civilizations. An outsider to such studies like myself may refer in this connection to the book entitled *The Intellectual Adventure of Ancient Man,*[1] in which specialists in the study of ancient civilizations tell us of these fruits. There John Wilson explains that the Egyptian inscription known as the Memphite Theology shows the reflective mind working out an adjustment between older and more widely held views as to the origin of the world and the powers of the gods and views appropriate to the rising importance of Memphis. The text, says Wilson, is a theological argument that Ptah, rather than the sun-god, was the primal god, and that Memphis was the center of the world. But more than this, in working out this reinterpretation of religious tradition, the priests of Memphis, says Wilson, subsumed the variant ideas under a higher philosophy. In place of the older idea of the creation of the world in such physical terms as, say, the Maori also conceived it, as separation of earth from sky, these Egyptian priests related creation to the processes of thought and speech and so anticipated the Book of Genesis.

In the same book, Thorkild Jacobsen's interesting discussion of the Gilgamesh epic shows systematization and also growing skepticism among the ancient Mesopotamians. This epic Jacobsen finds was composed around the beginning of the second millennium be-

[1] H. and H. A. Frankfort et al., *The Intellectual Adventure of Ancient Man* (Chicago, 1946).—Ed.

fore Christ out of older stories woven into a new whole. It is a work of synthesis, of reflective adjustment of parts to make a work philosophically coherent. The later work is no mere chronicle of primitive creation, episode by episode. Its theme is death, and it asks the great question as to why the good must die. A later Mesopotamian document, known as "The Dialogue of Pessimism," foreshadows Ecclesiastes, for in this ancient composition love, charity, and piety are one-by-one examined and found empty; the conclusion is reached that good and evil alike will be forgotten and so be indistinguishable. This is a development of speculative thought, hinted at only in the words of the African native or the Sioux Indian, but now, in an ancient civilization, carried far forward in the direction of a skeptical philosophy. These examples are enough to remind us that civilization is the cultivation of our more ultimate purposes. By the folk the moral order is, on the whole, taken as given. There only a few people are able to ask the great questions, or can look with doubt and intellectual challenge at what is for most men all of the time taken for granted; and, without writing, what these few minds accomplish leaves little residue. But the first cities bring a literate elite and a new freedom of the mind to criticize and to record. Then the moral order, though it is shaken by civilization, is also, in civilization, taken by reason into charge.

The moral order in early civilization is taken in charge by specialists as a philosophical problem. But this is not to say that it is taken in charge as a program for action. The little sketch of the development of the speculative mind which I have given brings us to a freer and more creative kind of thinking than could have existed in precivilized societies. It does not show us man undertaking to change his world and himself. Let us return to the societies known to ethnologists for what light they may shed on reform in the human community before the first civilizations.

The important statement that is generally true and relevant here is that in primitive societies uninfluenced by civilization the future is seen as a reproduction of the immediate past. Men see their children doing on the whole what they did themselves and are satisfied to see them doing so. The fortunes of individual men and women may rise or fall; calamity may strike one man or everybody, and success may or may not come; but the ways of life, the things to try for and to realize, remain the same.

The point is made plainer when one looks at the institutions by which civilized men sometimes seek to change their world to see whether or not these same institutions are used for such a purpose in primitive societies. The answer is, of course, that they are not. Consider education, and consider what the sociologist calls "voluntary associations." These two institutions have for their function in primitive societies—and hence, I am asserting, in precivilized societies—the reproduction of the current mode of life. They do not, as in our own society, take on also the function of changing the current mode of life in some direction of intended change.

It is now abundantly demonstrated that in many a primitive society there is education in the sense of conscious effort of adults to influence the behavior of children and younger people in directions which the adults think desirable. The direction is a repetition of the adults' way of life. Studies of primitive education which I have read make other points about that education: that moral instruction is its core; that it sometimes strives to recognize special abilities of individuals and is modified to fit; that the techniques of instruction are often well adapted to their ends. But it may be safely said that during all of human history until recent times the end of education has been to make, by education, the sort of adult that is admired in the society in which the teacher himself grew up and to make the child ready for a world like that in which the teacher lives. Margaret Mead has put the contrast between primitive education and modern Western education so clearly that I can do no better than to quote her words.

> Primitive education was a process by which continuity was maintained between parents and children. . . . Modern education includes a heavy emphasis upon the function of education to create discontinuities—to turn the child of the peasant into a clerk, the farmer into a lawyer, of the Italian immigrant into an American, of the illiterate into the literate.

And also: "Education becomes a mechanism of change." The belief has grown up in America "that it was possible by education to build a new world—a world that no man had yet dreamed . . . that we can bring up our children . . . to be equipped as we never were equipped." Nor does Dr. Mead neglect to mention the conflicts that result in our kind of civilized society between the more popular and widespread desire to use education to keep things as they are, and the desire of some modern people to build a new and better world with it. This very new dimension of education is a development of modern civilization. I do not know if the disposition to change society by changing one's children appears at all in the ancient civilizations; I should doubt it. Here we are talking of one of the later aspects of what perhaps we might speak of as the transforming advent of reform.

Nor shall we find the beginnings of reform in the secret societies and other associations of the primitive peoples. . . . The most that the ethnographic materials suggest as to the possible relation of associations to the idea of reform is that from a conflict of interests within a primitive society the purposes of one group in its struggle for power with another might have stimulated the formulation of programs of action. Ralph Linton tells us that after the Comanche Indians moved out onto the Plains, the young men of the tribe, organized into age grades with strong *esprit de corps,* exhibited marked disrespect of their elders. Perhaps out of such conflict a struggle for authority might develop which would make the young men and the old men two contending factions within the society. And a faction is a political group, a group that commonly develops a plan and a policy. But this is speculation; I find no real evidence that it happened among the Comanche. I think that if we are to look for the development of explicit programs of social change in pre-civilized societies, it is in these situations of conflicting special interest that we are likely to find it, if at all. Primitive societies are certainly not altogether static; changing environmental circumstances, meetings with other peoples, and the very variety of viewpoint and interest which exists even in a small homogeneous group are factors that stimulate change. But we are here not looking for the roots of social change; we seek the origins of the concept of reform.

On the whole, I think that neither the primitive societies nor the ancient civilized societies show us, except rarely, the phenomenon of conscious reform in their institutions. It is not easy for men to adopt the explicit position that it is their work to make over human living. Ancient reformers speak as if they were restoring the purity of the past. An announced purpose to change things in such a way as to make a society different from what had ever been before is probably unimportant in Western history until quite modern times, and even there begins gradually, with the writing of Utopias, the fanciful projection of alternative states of society, and reorganizations of society after periods of war or other disorder. In China, where the mode of life was relatively so self-contained for so long, the revolutionary purpose, except for the Ch'in period, is not to be noted until very recent times. Even in modern civilized societies most of the associations which men and women join exist to carry on some function, or realize some interest that on the whole maintains the existing state of affairs. . . .

I say again that in primitive and in precivilized societies, the minds of men look to a future that reproduces the immediate past. Yet in a time of great crisis the minds of men imagine a future that is different from the past. Reform has two parts: a vision of an altered future, and a program for reaching it. It is the vision, the dream, that comes easier to a people. It takes longer in the human career for people to formulate and adopt programs of reforming action. . . . The spirit of reform, the making of man's world by man's design, which makes civilization so different a thing from precivilized living, begins with the dreaming of the great revolutionary dreams.

Does it also begin in an immediate act? May we find, in primitive society, man not as a dreamer of a new world, but man as a pragmatic reformer, man exerting himself here and now to change the world around him nearer to his desires?

It is clear that in the early civilizations, where a variety of ideas and views of life are brought into competitive stimulation of one another, and where power is gathered into the hands of a single ruler, sweeping reforms may be at least attempted. One thinks again of the attempt of Amenhotep IV (Akhnaton)[2] to impose on Egypt the cult of Aton, and of the burning of the Confucian books under Shih Huang Ti.[3] And, on the side of the common people, civilization provides at least that discontent that may generate reform; strikes of workers and rebellions of subject peoples were certainly not unknown in the ancient civilizations. But we are just now looking at the peoples never civilized to see if we can find among them that essentially civilized and especially modern type, the reformer.

The abolition of the ancient taboos in Hawaii in the year 1819 was

[2] Amenhotep IV, also known as Akhnaton, was king of Egypt from 1375–1358 B.C. and a religious reformer.—Ed.
[3] Shih Huang Ti was emperor of China from 246–210 B.C. and builder of the Great Wall.—Ed.

certainly a sweeping reform, and it occurred among people who were not, in the usual sense, civilized. The event was, to most of the Hawaiian people, far from gradual; it was catastrophic. One day, in sight of the people, the ladies of the royal family ate forbidden foods, and then—abomination to the old gods—the king came over and ate publicly with the women. So drastic a violation of sacred custom was this that the people realized, however they felt about it, that the taboos were permanently broken and the old gods overthrown. The high priest himself destroyed his temple.

Were Kaahumanu and her fellow conspirators reformers? It seems plain that they were. They intended to overthrow a system both religious and political, and they accomplished their end. But when we ask if the reform would have been even attempted had the civilization of the white man not come into the South Seas, we ask a question that is unanswerable but that raises doubts that the reform would have then been attempted in the absence of influences from civilization. Although the event occurred five months before the first Christian missionaries landed, the Hawaiians for forty years had been getting—and appreciating—the weapons, cloth, and other material goods of the white man. Kamehameha I had two trusted white advisors. The first missionaries to arrive in Hawaii were received by royal ladies dressed in European style. Liholiho, the ruling chief at that time, was already living in a European kind of house. He and his father had built his conquests with European weapons and European advice. Ship captains had had to fight off bold young Hawaiians who were eager to join the crew and see the world. There is evidence that the Hawaiians had heard of the overthrow of native religion already accomplished in Tahiti. Before the missionaries reached Hawaii, two Hawaiians who were not "taboo chiefs" had had themselves baptized Christians by the chaplain of a French ship. So it is quite plain that the prestige of the white man and even of his religion had affected Hawaiians before the overthrow of the taboo. Moreover, the introduction of the white man's weapons had intensified the struggles between family groups, some of which were anti-taboo, and the new trade in sandalwood had placed new strains on the social and political system. These are all elements in the situation which suggest that influence from the whites brought about the great reform. On the other hand, the native mode of life included some features, apart from white influence, which plainly made it easier for this reform to succeed should it be attempted. Among these features were the inconsistency between the high position of certain women in the system of political power and the low position of these women as women, as expressed in the taboos; the habituation of the Hawaiians, like other Polynesians, to the desertion of their gods; "the acceptance of a more powerful god as a means of obtaining spiritual power was a common Polynesian characteristic"; and, of course, the personal interests that those disadvantaged by the taboo system had in doing away with it. Kroeber's view[4] that the main factor was "a kind of social staleness," that the Hawaiians were simply tired of their religion, may be right; but such an interpretation has to be considered together with the evidence that young Hawaiians, stimulated by white contacts and new opportunities to travel and trade, were inclined to try the new as much as to give up the old. The strict conclusion is that this Hawaiian reform is not a case of a reform accomplished quite outside of or before civilization. It occurred on the margins of the expanding white man's civilization. It took place among a people whose primitive mode of life included, in addition to the elements favoring change that I have already mentioned, one of the elements which in civilized societies helps to make reform achievable, marked concentration of political power. . . .

The strongest impression is that in societies unaffected by civilization men change their ideas and their ways of doing things, and are not infrequently aware that they are doing so, but that under conditions of isolation these changes are small changes. The reach into the future to make life different from what it was is a short reach. And the reach occurs when some immediate circumstances present the people with a difficulty. . . . Most of the changes in making rules for the conduct of a simple society probably occurred also in the course of meeting particular new situations in which the old rules could not be simply applied. . . .

On the other hand, to recognize this common humanity of problem-seeing and problem-solving is not to say that primitive man was conspicuously a reformer. Of course he was not. Until the coming of civilization men were used to expecting the future to be like what they had themselves experienced, and their institutions kept things running; they did not exist to make life over.

[4] A. L. Kroeber, an American anthropologist noted for his seminal contributions to physical anthropology, archaeology, and ethnology.—Ed.

But the human nature was the same, and men in primitive societies can readily turn to the future and conceive it to be made different from the past, if events require that they do so. The turning of the prospective myth forward in a crisis, at a time when the old ways of life are broken and have become unserviceable, shows that this is so. I was myself struck with the rapidity with which certain Maya Indians living in isolated villages in Yucatan adopted the idea of reform, the notion that they would make over at least the material conditions of their lives, when the spirit of the Mexican revolution of 1917–1921 reached them far out in the bush. Where the fathers in the home community had conserved ancient tradition, the sons, out in a new settlement, decided, very conscious of what they were doing, to build a healthier and more prosperous life. Progress is rapidly contagious. There is nothing in the natural capacities of primitive people to prevent them from taking the idea almost instantly.

It is plain that civilization provides the circumstances in which these capacities to build a new future are demanded and so come into development. Civilization is breakdown of old ways. It is a meeting of many minds. It is the weight of new exactions upon human labor; and it is the organization and mass production of food, buildings, war, cruelty, and political adventure. The reformer is not likely to arise nor to be welcomed in a society where everybody does much the same thing and young people go on doing what old people did. The reformer, in Professor Schlesinger's apt phrase is "a disturber of the peace."[5] But what if the peace is already disturbed? It is always disturbed, for many people, in civilization. Then the reformer strives to change the world, already so troubled, or to change the people in it.

Primitive people are potential but not actual reformers.

[5] Reference here is to Arthur M. Schlesinger's *The American Reformer* (Cambridge, 1950).—Ed.

Robert McC. Adams
SOCIAL STRATIFICATION AND THE ADVENT OF CIVILIZATION

Still another criticism of the "Childe thesis" involves his use of the term "Urban Revolution" and his excessive stress on technological and subsistence patterns as the key to the rise of civilization. Robert McC. Adams cautions the reader that the word "revolution" may conjure up images of the early urban development that are more dramatic than the facts allow. He also believes that social stratification was far more crucial to the advent of civilization than technological change had been. Adams has been on the staff of the Oriental Institute at the University of Chicago since 1955 and is a former director of the institute. He has conducted archaeological fieldwork both in the Near East and Mexico.

There is no need to dwell at length on definitions of the entities with which this study deals. The major characteristics of early states have been repeatedly described, and in any case I am more concerned with the *process* of their growth than with a detailed discussion of their characteristics. There is no more adequate term evoking this process than that introduced by V. Gordon Childe, the "Urban Revolution." Among its important advantages are that it places stress on the transformative character of the change, that it suggests at least relative rapidity, and that it specifies a restricted, urban locus within which the process was concentrated.

Yet it must be admitted that there are potential distortions involved in the use of the term as well as advantages, quite apart from the specific attributes Childe attaches to it. The more common usage of the word "revolution," for example, implies aspects of conscious struggle. Possibly there were overtones of consciousness about certain stages or aspects of the Urban Revolution, although the issue is unsettled. Any implication that such was generally the case, however, is certainly false. Again, the term perhaps implies a uniform emphasis on the growth of the city as the core of the process. At least as a form of settlement, however, urbanism seems to have been much less important to the emergence of the state, and even to the development of civilization in the broadest sense, than social stratification and the institutionalization of political authority.

Still a further possible drawback is that uncritical use of the term may invoke an implicit, and therefore dangerous, assumption of the unity of all urban phenomena. This is at best a proposition that applies at so gross a level as to be hardly more than trivial, and yet it sometimes has served to divert attention toward misleading analogies with other cultural settings sharing only the fact of settlement in dense, "urban" clusters rather than toward the empirical investigation of the phenomena in hand. In short, the purpose of this study emphatically is not to generalize about the nature of cities but rather to discuss the processes by which, at least in some cases, they seem first to have come into existence. And as will become apparent, the achievement of these first steps in urban growth leads to a distinctive constellation of features that cannot be regarded simply as progressively approximating contemporary urbanism more and more closely.

In balance, the insights engendered by the term seem to outweigh its drawbacks. But the characteristics with which Childe sought to describe and associate it are less satisfactory. His criteria were the following: (1) increase in settlement size toward "urban" proportions; (2) centralized accumulation of capital resulting from the imposition of tribute or taxation; (3) monumental public works; (4) the invention of writing; (5) advances toward exact and predictive sciences; (6) the appearance and growth of long-distance trade in luxuries; (7) the emergence of a class-stratified society; (8) the freeing of a part of the population from subsistence tasks for full-time craft specialization; (9) the substitution of a politically organized society based on territorial principles, the state, for one based on kin ties; and (10) the appearance of naturalistic—or perhaps better, representational—art.

One objection to such a listing is that it gives us a mixed bag of characteristics. Some, like monumental architecture, can be unequivocally documented from archaeological evidence but also are known to have been associated occasionally with noncivilized peoples. Others, like exact and predictive sciences, are largely matters of interpretation from evidence that is at best fragmentary and ambiguous. And still others, if not most of Childe's criteria, obviously must have emerged through a gradual, cumulative process not easily permitting distinctions in kind to be kept apart from those merely in degree. Moreover, these characteristics differ radically from one another in their importance as causes, or even as indices, of the Urban Revolution as a whole. The significance of the reappearance of representational art—indeed, its initial appearance, insofar as it deals with the human figure—for example, is at least not immediately apparent.

A more basic objection to any such listing is that its electicism embraces fundamental contradictions as to purpose. Childe echoes Morgan[1] in seeking to identify the Urban Revolution by a series of traits whose vestiges the specialist can conveniently recognize. This was a reasonable procedure for Morgan's purpose, the initial delineation of a succession of stages, but with Childe, on the other hand, we enter an era in which the emphasis shifted toward providing accounts with explanatory power as well.

The term "Urban Revolution" implies a focus on ordered, systematic *processes* of change through time. Hence the identifying characteristics of the Urban Revolution need to be more than loosely associated features (no matter how conveniently recognizable), whose functional role is merely assumed and which are defined in terms of simple presence or absence. Usefully to speak of an Urban Revolution, we must describe a functionally related core of institutions as they interacted and evolved through time. From this viewpoint, the characteristics Childe adduces can be divided into a group of primary variables, on the one hand, and a larger group of secondary, dependent variables, on the other. And it clearly was Childe's view that the primary motivating forces for the transformation lay in the rise of new technological and subsistence patterns. The accumulative growth of technology and the increasing availability of food surpluses as deployable capital, he argued, were the central causative agencies underlying the Urban Revolution.

This study is somewhat differently oriented; it tends to stress "societal" variables rather than "cultural" ones. Perhaps in part, such an approach is merely an outgrowth of limitations of space; social institutions lend themselves more easily to the construction

[1] Lewis Henry Morgan (1818–1881), the father of American anthropology, ethnologist, and authority on American Indians. Morgan wrote one of the first ethnologies and made an early attempt to grapple with the idea of universal principles of cultural evolution.—Ed.

of a brief paradigm than do the tool types or pottery styles with which the archaeologist traditionally works. But I also believe that the available evidence supports the conclusion that the transformation at the core of the Urban Revolution lay in the realm of social organization. And, while the onset of the transformation obviously cannot be understood apart from its cultural and ecological context, it seems to have been primarily changes in social institutions that precipitated changes in technology, subsistence, and other aspects of the wider cultural realm, such as religion, rather than vice versa. . . .

*   *   *

. . . What is our evidence for the development of social stratification? What forms did it take in our respective areas? Can we identify a common structure of stratification beneath the welter of divergent local features? Of course, this problem is complicated by the fact that we are dealing with relatively "primitive," undifferentiated systems in which social stratification did not develop as an autonomous, distinctive feature but was "embedded" in multifunctional institutions embracing political and religious components as well. But I believe it remains a valid analytical entity, and without such entities essays in comparison like this one could consist only of contrasting social systems as descriptively integrated wholes—and hence would be foredoomed.

To begin with early Mesopotamia, the available evidence takes a succession of forms which influence the interpretations that can be made of it. In the late Ubaid period,[2] apparently the "take-off" point for the Urban Revolution, it consists almost exclusively of reports from excavations in cemeteries, for example, more than two hundred graves excavated at Eridu, as well as others at Ur and al-Ubaid. Differentiation in grave wealth cannot necessarily be linked directly to differences in status, at least in the absence of converging lines of inference from other evidence. It is therefore fortunate that the broad trend toward increasing differentiation disclosed by later graves from Khafajah, Kish, Jemdet Nasr, Shuruppak, and, above all, Ur can be at first supplemented and confirmed, and ultimately over-

[2] The Ubaid period (c. 4400–3500 B.C.) witnessed the spread of "Ubaid Culture," originally centered in southern Iraq, over the whole of Mesopotamia. This development laid the foundation for Sumerian civilization, and Mesopotamia became the center of the civilized Near East.—Ed.

shadowed, by textual and archaeological evidence on aspects of social differentiation other than those associated with mortuary practices.

In the late Ubaid period significant differentiation in grave wealth was almost entirely absent. Normal grave furniture consisted of one or more pottery vessels placed near the feet, with, in some cases, the substitution of stone vessels for those of clay and the occasional addition of pottery figurines and of decorative bands of beads on the clothing of the deceased. In the Warka and Protoliterate periods greater variation begins to be apparent. Stone maceheads, a copper spear-point, and greater numbers of stone vessels are attested. About one-third of the 25 graves beneath the floors of late Protoliterate private houses at Khafajah were accompanied by stone bowls, and two contained somewhat larger (although still modest) accumulations, including a few well-made vessels of copper, lead, and stone, as well as the usual pottery.

A much larger number of graves of roughly Protoliterate date have been excavated at Ur, although unfortunately the chronological placement of many of them is somewhat doubtful. Of the 340 or so that have been described, less than 10 percent contain only pottery, while 61 contain one or two simple lead cups or other metal objects. Only 2 graves of this large series suggest substantial concentrations of wealth, and in both cases the accompanying pottery implies a somewhat later date than the excavator attributes to them. Both contain beads and ornaments of carnelian and lapis lazuli, a few copper and lead bowls and other utensils, considerable numbers of stone vessels, and, of course, pottery. On the assumption that they may be assigned only to the very end of the Protoliterate period at the earliest, they suggest the beginnings of a trend toward increasing differentiation but certainly do not indicate that processes of social stratification had as yet proceeded very far.

With the advent of writing and representational art in the Protoliterate period, the picture can be somewhat sharpened and amplified. Signs already appear for "slave girl" among the earliest Protoliterate tablets, while that for "male slave" seemingly occurs slightly later. The term for "slave" is a derivative from an expression for "foreign country," perhaps suggesting that the institution originated either in the taking of war captives or in the impressment of seminomadic groups who drifted into the settlements after their herds fell below an acceptable minimum for subsistence. Bound "war captives" apparently are shown on a celebrated seal impression from Uruk, although it may be significant that male slaves appear not only later but also in far smaller numbers than do female ones. Possibly the means for the retention and effective employment of male captives had not yet been worked out, so that they were generally killed. Unfortunately, the functional basis for the institution of slavery at the time cannot be determined from the poorly understood texts. Nor are we justified in uncritically inferring that the complex, fully crystallized patterns of the late Early Dynastic period[3] were already present merely on the basis of the occurrence of the terms.

Other contemporary gradations of status are even less clear. There are imposing representations of priests and "king"-like figures, but in general they create more questions than they answer: What portion of the conceptual continuum between mythopoeic thought and "reality" do they portray? Do they illustrate "events" or rituals? And, if mainly rituals, as seems likely, do the apparent importance and specialized roles of individuals within that context necessarily reflect their general status as well? At any event, since we must postpone the discussion of specific political and religious functions, . . . it can be noted here only that representational art possibly does reflect some of the attributes and activities of new elites that would not be known from the available reports of cemeteries in spite of the fairly large number of graves that have been excavated.

As a perhaps significant bit of negative evidence, it may be noted that the terms lu, "full, free citizen," and mash-en-kak, perhaps "commoner of subordinate status," other major components of Mesopotamian society in historic times, do not occur in any presently known documents before the Early Dynastic period. In spite of the presence of terms for "slave," in other words, there is still no unequivocal evidence for the emergence of a fully developed system of class distinctions at least until the onset of the Early Dynastic period.

By late Early Dynastic times there is much fuller and less ambiguous evidence to suggest the existence of just such a system. It can best be documented, of course, from contemporary written records, but to rely on them alone would overemphasize the contrasts with earlier periods for which they were not available, thus perhaps also

---

[3] The Early Dynastic period of Sumerian civilization began around 3000 B.C. and lasted for approximately 500 years. The Early Dynastic sequence has been divided into three stages, I–III, to reflect the continuity in material progress.—Ed.

overstressing the disjunctive aspects of change during the Early Dynastic period. So let us consider first the archaeological evidence.

Architectural exposures sufficiently large to provide a meaningful picture of differentiation in private domestic architecture occur only in the Diyala area east of modern Baghdad. To judge from ancient Eshnunna, the larger houses lay along the main roads through the settlement and often occupied 200 square meters or more of floor area. The greater number of houses, on the other hand, were considerably smaller and seem to have been compressed into the interiors of the "blocks" formed by the main streets and the establishments adjoining them, having access to the arterial roads only by means of twisting, narrow alleys. As a result, many of the smaller houses lack the characteristic enclosed court of Mesopotamia houses in general and do not exceed 50 square meters of total area. There is independent evidence in the associated small finds, in one case consisting of a valuable hoard, that the large houses were occupied by persons of greater wealth as well as superior status. Significantly, the largest dwelling was apparently that of a merchant, for opening on the street from the residence behind was a display room with tiers of bins and receptacles.

The impression of differentiation is confirmed and amplified by a study of tomb furniture. One of the clearest indices to wealth is the presence of copper, as well as more precious metals. In part, the increasing quantities of copper found in Early Dynastic graves may reflect only an enlargement in supplies reaching the lowland cities, but the previously unparalleled concentrations of metal that appear in a few graves nonetheless must indicate a correspondingly increased range of differentiation in wealth. And while copper becomes *"le métal d'échange par excellence"* by the Early Dynastic III period, on the whole it remained of so high a value that ordinary craftsmen and even minor bureaucrats were limited to at most a few implements of this material for which they were at pains to keep an accounting. The bulk of the peasantry may not have benefited from the increasing supplies at all, for none of the utilitarian copper implements connected with agriculture that have been recovered so far apparently was made earlier than the Akkadian period. In other words, copper implements and vessels (to say nothing of gold or silver) qualitatively increase the implication of wealth for the burial assemblages in which they occur, as opposed to those in which they are lacking.

In the Early Dynastic I period, there already was greater variation in the kind and amount of accompanying grave goods than had occurred previously. At Kish, for example, burial equipment for the ordinary grave still consisted of a few large spouted jars and other pottery vessels, with no weapons or ornaments; but an unspecified, presumably small, number of graves contained copper daggers, lances, axes, sling missiles, stone and copper vessels, copper mirrors and toilet articles, and the like. Although not representing great concentrations of wealth when compared with the royal tombs, the luxury character of many of the burial offerings is evident. There are copper stands or trellis supports, for example, which are found exclusively in association with stone vessels in some of the wealthier burials. At contemporary rates of exchange, the weight of copper wire in the trellises would have been sufficient to purchase a field large enough to provide a modest livelihood, yet each of the stone vessels found in a support could stand unaided.

A somewhat later development roughly corresponds with the late Early Dynastic II and III periods. It is known most spectacularly from the so-called "Royal Cemetery" at Ur, although contemporary finds at Kish and Khafajah confirm the same general pattern and provide some hundreds of additional graves as examples. At Ur, 588 burials have been described that were not connected with "royal tombs." Of them, about one-eighth lacked metal or stone objects of any kind, while an additional 751 graves, although they yielded no offerings suitable for dating, must be roughly coeval with them. Here we see the remains of a peasantry presumably maintaining itself only slightly above the margins of subsistence, physically associated with an urban center but having acquired few of the tangible symbols of its wealth or technological progress.

On the other hand, about twenty seemingly non-"royal" graves contain a substantial wealth of offerings: personal ornaments of gold and silver, large numbers of well-made stone and copper vessels, beads of gold and lapis lazuli, gold bowls, gold- and silver-mounted daggers, quantities of bronze tools and weapons, etc. Below this extreme, but intergrading with it to form a relatively smooth curve of distribution, were considerably more numerous graves that, on the average, contained several copper and bronze tools and utensils (mirrors, strainers, razors, bowls, axes) in addition to pottery, an assortment which Sir Leonard Woolley[4] somewhat offhandedly characterizes as "typical middle class." In all, 434 of the graves at Ur have some metal and 167 have objects of gold and silver, a very high proportion of the 588 clearly datable graves and a respectable proportion of the total even if all the undated graves are assumed to be contemporary.

In sum, insofar as grave goods reflect the general distribution of wealth, there is evidence for a decisive increase in social differentiation in the cities during the course of the Early Dynastic period. It did not take the form of a numerous elite that was sharply cut off from an undifferentiated mass of artisans and peasantry. Instead, it appears that the resources of the royal family frequently were only slightly superior to those of a few great private houses and that in the main urban centers the latter, in turn, graded off gradually to various degrees of impoverishment.

It is interesting to contrast this concentration of wealth at Ur with the situation obtaining in the contemporary, nearby site of al-Ubaid. Of 94 recorded burials there, only 18 contained any metal at all, only 4 contained more than a single metal object, only 1 contained objects of precious metal, and no grave contained more than 3 metal objects. Al-Ubaid, it would seem, was a rural dependency of the capital at Ur, with much of its wealth drained off to support urban specialists and administrators.

Whether this was generally the case with the rural population—and, indeed, how much of the population lived in outlying, dependent villages—is a question that cannot be answered, in view of the exclusive concern of Mesopotamian archaeology heretofore with the greater aesthetic appeal, and greater promise of finding texts, in the cities. Large numbers of villages do occur in the northern part of the alluvium, but that region, Akkad, differs both culturally and ecologically from the region of Sumer in which most of the classical Sumerian city-states were located. There are textual references to temporary structures near the fields that were occupied by Sumerian agricultural workers during the harvest season, and it is at least

---

[4] Sir Leonard Woolley (1880–1960) was a very prominent British archaeologist. One of his greatest contributions was the discovery of the city of Ur in southern Mesopotamia, proving it was not a mythical city as many authorities had believed. —Ed.

possible that many small settlements like al-Ubaid were consolidated into larger, more defensible urban centers either just before or during the Early Dynastic period. On the other hand, several centuries later than the Early Dynastic period, the little Sumerian kingdom of Lagash is reported to have comprised some 25 towns and 40 or more villages and hamlets within a 1,600 square kilometer area. If so, something of the same pattern may have persisted from Protoliterate or earlier times right through and beyond the initial impulses toward urbanization.

The conclusion from the archaeological evidence that late Early Dynastic society was a stratified, class system is confirmed and amplified by the contemporary written records. At least its quantitative characteristics can be best understood by a study of differences in ownership or control of land, but the Shuruppak and Lagash archives also provide information on some of the duties, perquisites, and relative positions of the various strata.

At the bottom of the social hierarchy were slaves, individuals who could be bought and sold and who seemingly were owned in small numbers even by some ordinary artisans, agriculturalists, and minor administrators. Their economic role was a much more significant one, however, in connection with great estates and temples, of which the Bau archive furnishes so richly documented an example. In the Bau community of some 1,200 persons, there were from 250 to 300 slaves, of whom the overwhelming proportion were women. One tablet alone lists 205 slave girls and their children who probably were employed in a centralized weaving establishment like one known archaeologically at the site of ancient Eshnunna; other women are known to have been engaged in milling, brewing, cooking, and similar interior operations permitting close supervision. Male slaves generally are referred to as igi-nu-du, "the blind ones," and apparently were employed in gardening operations. Although there are no direct references to the blinding of war prisoners to prevent their escape, it is a possibility that at least remains open.

While it has sometimes been maintained that slavery as an institution was of minor, almost insignificant, importance in ancient Mesopotamia, there are two respects in which this view must be contradicted. In the first place, even if the gross proportion of slaves was relatively small, we have just noted that their distribution throughout the economy was highly uneven. In the Bau archive, representing a great estate or temple, perhaps one-sixth of all resources available above the subsistence level were devoted to the production of wool and thread. Moreover, slaves working under semi-industrialized conditions played a preponderant part in this process, and the sale or exchange of this commodity not only played an important part in the local redistributive economy but presumably also served as the basis for long-distance trade in luxuries and vital raw materials like metal. In a sense then, there was a strategic concentration of slaves in precisely those institutions which characterized Mesopotamian urban society as distinguished from preurban society, so to characterize the institution as insignificant, accordingly would misrepresent its importance as a factor in development.

A second argument for the strategic importance of slavery has recently been persuasively elaborated by Moses Finley.[5] His essential point is that the data from the Old World, both Near Eastern and Classical, does not reflect a polarization of society into slaves and free citizens but, instead, a wide spectrum of alternative possibilities. Legal, social, political, and economic criteria of dependence or subservience may overlap and contradict one another, but there was a cumulative movement until Classical times toward more and more sharply defining and isolating a dependent stratum of foreigners at the bottom of the social hierarchy. In fact, it is only with this development that the abstract contrast of "slavery" with "freedom" emerged at all.

The implication of Finley's analysis for our present problem is that it is perhaps inapropos to reserve the term "slavery" for the group I have just discussed, on the implicit assumption that it is sharply contrasted with a much larger "free" population. Instead, there were various social impediments and conditions of servitude, of which slavery was merely the most extreme, and the role of an inferior and in some respects unfree agricultural class was surely far more important than the numbers of narrowly defined "slaves" alone would suggest. Seen in this light, the controversy between Soviet economic historians characterizing early state society as "slave" society and Western specialists insisting on the relatively small numbers of slaves in some respects becomes more a matter of nomenclature than of substance.

[5] Here Adams refers to Moses I. Finley, "Between Slavery and Freedom," *Comparative Studies in Society and History* 6 (1964): 233–249.—Ed.

The so-called "shub-lugals," of whom there were about eighty in the Bau community organized in groups under overseers or foremen, are an example of a group with a reduced status and degree of freedom. The term has been variously translated as "subjects of the king" or merely as "subjects of a master," but in any case their clientage is apparent from their duties. In various texts they are reported as laboring in gangs by the day on demesne lands of the Bau temple or estate, pulling ships, digging irrigation canals, and serving as a nucleus of the city militia (perhaps specialized slingers or archers) under the direct command of the palace administration. Two muster rolls that have been preserved make it clear that upon the death of a shub-lugal he was succeeded by a near relative, who assumed his same duties under the same overseer. By the time of the Bau archive at about the end of the Early Dynastic period, shub-lugals were among many groups who received a subsistence ration during four months of the year in return for labor service. The shub-lugals also were allotted small plots of prebendal land from holdings of the temple or estate. There are indications that further control over the group was maintained by the periodic reallocation of the plots, even though their size indicates that many of them would have been inadequate for subsistence purposes.

There are other groups that basically resemble the shub-lugals, although differing in their economic position and apparent degree of clientage. The uku-ush, who perhaps served as heavily armed shield- and spear-bearing units in the phalanx formations of the army, also served as overseers for the shub-lugals on labor assignments but were bound by approximately the same conditions of service. More ambiguous are the positions of engars and sag-apins. Engars have been described variously as "clients" and "free peasants," but in any case both titles can at least be assigned somewhat higher positions in the social hierarchy; they conducted or supervised agricultural operations on behalf of the estate or temple, supplied cadres for the militia, and received both rations and allotments of prebendal land. None of these groups could be bought or sold, it must be stressed, although the clientage of a number of shub-lugals in Lagash may have been involuntarily transferred from the city ruler Lugalanda to his successor, Urukagina.

Clearly, there was not a single status of clientage but a series of perhaps overlapping ones based on distinctions that are not yet apparent. And it is admittedly dangerous to generalize from the limited and selective archival sources at present available, particularly in view of their disproportionate emphasis on the larger (especially temple and palace) estates with scribes in their employ and special managerial problems for which permanent accounts were almost a necessity. If Diakonoff's[6] estimate is correct, as much as two-thirds of the population in late Early Dynastic times still was not directly dependent on manorial units at all but was organized instead in corporate kin communities. However, it does seem reasonable to conclude that at least on agricultural estates the labor force consisted primarily of this semifree gurush class, whom I. J. Gelb[7] has likened to Greek *metoikoi,* Roman *glebae adscripti,* and English serfs.

Even on lands apparently not falling within the bounds of great temples and estates, there are suggestions that small private plots were not held in alodial tenure but were subject to certain forms of entailment. They could be sold and transferred, as we know from many examples at Shuruppak, but nevertheless they stood in some relationship to a superordinate institution—probably the administrative establishment of the city ruler. Plows and even seed corn were provided by this central authority, a practice that apparently can be traced back as far as Protoliterate times on the basis of a tablet of that date from Tell Uqair. The notarization of a dub-sar-gan (field scribe), who must have been a representative of this establishment, was an integral part of every purchase contract. Moreover, it may be noted that sales occur in rigid multiples of 2.5 iku (0.88 hectare). One might suspect on this basis that sales were not entirely at the discretion of the individual owners but were subject to a degree of superordinate control that the documents took for granted and therefore do not mention.

Large-scale private acquisitions of land have already been mentioned. Perhaps the earliest example known is the so-called "Blau Monument," long regarded as a forgery prior to the discovery of pictographic Protoliterate writing in secure archeological contexts. The purchase of 250 or more hectares by one Du-si and of at least

---

[6] Igor Diakonoff, "Sale of Land in Pre-Sargonic Sumer," in *Papers Presented by the Soviet Delegation at the XXIII International Congress of Orientalist, Assyriology Section* (Moscow, 1954), p. 21.—Ed.
[7] Ignac J. Gelb, noted Assyriologist in the Oriental Institute, University of Chicago. —Ed.

114 hectares by Lu-pad, a high official of Umma, are later, better understood examples, while the acquisitions in four districts that are recorded by one Akkadian king on the "Obelisk of Manishtusu" total 2,300 hectares and those by Enhegal of Lagash amounted to about 1,000 hectares. Most if not all such purchases seem to have been made by members of ruling families or high officials, and the documents recording them are appropriately described as *"Sammelurkunden"*; that is, they are records not of the simple transfer of integrated large holdings but of the assembling of such holdings out of many separately owned, small parcels.

Thus the implication of an ongoing process of concentration of landownership in the hands of state officials during at least the later Early Dynastic and Akkadian periods cannot be doubted. In the case of the lands Manishtusu purchased, to be sure, they were redistributed to relatives and political supporters rather than being directly worked by their new owner. But that is unlikely to have been the case even with royal acquisitions before the wide conquests of the Akkadian period, and the king's correspondingly increased responsibilities for the defense of distant frontiers. And archives of a considerable number of Akkadian estates, privately owned and yet often employing on rations up to several hundred dependent agricultural workers and their families, make it clear that the trend in general was not toward redistribution but toward the growth of large, directly managed holdings.

Of a still larger order of magnitude than the acquisitions just cited were the estates already in the hands of the ruling officials of the palace and temple. The Bau archive is one of these, and in fact is the main source and prototype of Anton Deimel's reconstruction of an all-embracing *Tempelwirtschaft*. Now, as we have seen, Deimel's conclusion that units similar to the Bau temple virtually monopolized the available agricultural land has been shown to be untenable. Moreover, current studies even cast into some doubt his interpretation of the Bau community as subordinated in any significant way to the service of a particular god or a temple hierarchy. But Deimel's calculations of the total size of the establishment, about 65 square kilometers of arable land under the direction of an administrative official responsible to the wife of the Lagash city ruler, nevertheless seem entirely reasonable. Although much less is known of them, similar records of large landholdings can be traced back into the Protoliterate period; a fragmentary tablet from Jemdet Nasr accounts for 1,828 hectares and may have originally contained a much larger total.

Of course, the management of a manorial estate of this great size could not be fully centralized irrespective of whether it was conducted in religious or in secular terms. As we have seen, some of the estate lands were cultivated directly on its behalf by shub-lugals; on the basis of known proportions for a very small part of its area, the demesne lands might amount to about one-fourth of the total. Another, larger portion consisted of the prebendal lands allotted to members of the Bau community, the harvest from which presumably was devoted very largely to their own subsistence. By far the largest of such allotments was an area of some 348 hectares that also was cultivated on behalf of the city ruler and his wife by the shub-lugals, but, while other high officials also received generous amounts of land, most allotments were very small. Still a third portion consisted of rent lands, which were farmed on a share-crop basis, again largely by members of the Bau community, and which constitute almost half of the lands whose relative proportions can be accounted for.

Even the share-crop lands were centrally supplied with seed, draft animals, equipment, and specialized personnel for plowing. Moreover, accounts of receipts and disbursements suggest that about thirty storehouses were centrally managed—in one of which alone the presence of 9,450 tons of barley is recorded. Hence the Bau administration should not be construed as a political structure superimposed on a pattern of atomistically conducted agricultural operations merely to facilitate the passive collection of taxes or tribute. It was, in fact, an *oikos* in the classic Weberian sense, an authoritarian super-household in which a remarkably differentiated labor force of clients undertook to provide their lords with goods and services. Although little is known in detail of the earlier development of this integrated, consumption-oriented economy, it may be noted that the distribution of rations was already accounted for, presumably in exchange for labor services, as early as late Protoliterate times.

Drawing together the many diverse strands in this discussion of social stratification in early Mesopotamia, I believe we can trace the emergence of a fully developed class society by no later than the end of the Early Dynastic period. Its origins, prior to the appearance of cuneiform documents, can be followed only indirectly, in the gradual emergence of a difference between richly furnished tombs, on the one hand, and the much more numerous graves of a relatively impoverished peasantry, on the other. Subsequently, however, we can establish the internal gradations within this society more and more clearly from written sources. The system of stratification was, of course, closely articulated with systems of political and military powers and prerogatives, but those relationships must be reserved for consideration in the following chapter [of *The Evolution of Urban Society*]. . . .

Henry Bamford Parkes

THE THEOCRATIC BASIS OF CIVILIZATION

Another line that history has taken in seeking to explain the nature and significance of the advent of civilization is reflected in Henry Bamford Parkes's Gods and Men: The Origins of Western Culture. *Born in Sheffield, England and the descendant of a long line of Methodist ministers, Parkes is concerned with the theocratic aspects of early civilization. As the following selection will reveal, he believes that the technological advances, social stratification and other developments frequently associated with the rise of civilization would have been impossible without the leadership provided by priest-kings. Parkes has been a professor at New York University since 1930 and has published extensively on a variety of subjects.*

The areas where urban civilization was first superimposed upon the peasant base were Mesopotamia and Egypt, and the time was almost certainly the fourth millennium B.C. At subsequent periods, similar, and apparently independent, civilizations emerged in the valleys of the Indus and the Hoang-Ho, while several millennia later the same process occurred in Mexico and Peru, which by the fifteenth century of our era had reached a stage roughly equivalent to that of Mesopotamia and Egypt in the third millennium B.C. But the Euphrates and Nile valleys were the original sources of the civilization of

Western man. For the next three thousand years, in fact—more than half the total span of civilization in the Western world—its history remained the history of these two areas and of those surrounding regions, such as Syria, Anatolia, Iran, and the Mediterranean islands, that came under their influence.

The rise of a civilization was a complex process, dependent mainly on social and institutional changes rather than on any new technological discovery. Its most significant features were the unification of a number of peasant communities into some form of state, the government of which then had command of relatively large economic resources and supplies of manpower; the growth of the division of labor and the increase of classes with specialized functions not directly engaged in the production of food, such as priests, officials, craftsmen, and traders; and the building of cities largely inhabited by such classes. These developments were quickly followed by important cultural and economic advances, particularly by the invention of writing and the keeping of written records and by the use of metals, especially bronze. That this happened first in the valleys of the Euphrates and the Nile seems to have resulted from the need for artificial irrigation; human labor had to be organized for the building of canals that would control and conserve the summer floods of the rivers and distribute the water as widely as possible, and land and water rights had to be allotted to different village communities. This could be accomplished only under the direction of governments holding authority over relatively wide areas.

Man's first answer to the social and political problems involved in the rise of civilization was to strip himself of all responsibility for his own destiny and project all authority upon the gods. The priests who organized the building of irrigation canals and the establishment of central governments attributed their capacity for initiative and creativity to divine inspiration and demanded unquestioning obedience from their dependents on the ground that they were the vehicles of the divine will. Thus, the ancient city was a theocratic institution built around the temple of a tribal deity and ruled by a priest-king who was considered as his nominee and spokesman. In Mesopotamia each city was regarded as the property of its god, and the function of the human ruler was to serve as steward of the god's estates; according to Mesopotamian theology, men had been created in order to relieve the gods of the necessity of labor, and were therefore their slaves. In Egypt the king was actually himself a god, and hence was the owner of all the land and absolute master of all its inhabitants. Thus, the early civilizations were permeated with religion, finding their whole *raison d'être* in the service of heaven rather than of mankind, and maintaining order and unity by absolute obedience to the priest-kings in whom the will of heaven had become concentrated and embodied. In emerging from the protective shell of tribal tradition and confronting the anxieties of a more complex way of life, men sought security by maintaining a feeling of close and comprehensive dependence upon divine powers.

Theocratic civilization was hierarchical and authoritarian, and the beliefs upon which it was based were incompatible with the development of any understanding of scientific law or any concept of historical progress. As the gods were responsible for everything, all phenomena must be attributed to divine intervention rather than to natural causality; and as they had already fully expressed their will in the making of the world and the organization of human society, change was unreal and history meaningless. Man's happiness depended on conformity to the divine order embodied from the beginning in the institutions of the theocratic state. Theocratic principles, nevertheless, provided a workable solution to man's central political problem; by attributing earthly authority to divine appointment, they made it legitimate and gave it a right to unconditional loyalty. As long as faith in theocracy remained vital and unquestioning, the social order was organic and not mechanistic, being based on the willing consent of its members and not on coercion. After six thousand years men have not fully outgrown these theocratic attitudes and are still capable of reverting to them whenever they lose confidence in later and more rational concepts of political order.

For about one thousand years theocracy made possible a remarkable display of human energy and inventiveness. The centuries during which the Mesopotamian and Egyptian civilizations were first established, covering roughly the second half of the fourth millennium B.C. and the first half of the third, were one of the most creative epochs in all history. Having discovered a way of mobilizing and directing human skill and power on a much larger scale than had been possible in peasant society, the peoples of both these civilizations were responsible for astonishing achievements in almost all fields of human activity, most notably perhaps in mathematics, architecture and engineering, and the visual arts. This early efflorescence, however, was followed by a long period of cultural conservatism during which men consolidated and imitated the works of their predecessors and made few significant additions or innovations. Both the Mesopotamian and the Egyptian civilizations passed through epochs of breakdown and disintegration, with a consequent loss of faith in divine guidance; but men failed to affirm any alternative principle of political unity and could restore order only by reestablishing theocratic government, though with an increasing emphasis on military force and coercion. In fact, an interval of nearly two thousand years passed before the advent of another epoch of high creativity, and this developed not in Mesopotamia or Egypt, which were unable to break with their theocratic heritage, but among peoples with no previous tradition of civilization.

Priority in the building of civilization almost certainly belonged to the Sumerians, a people of unknown origin who had apparently first lived in mountainous country, perhaps in Iran, and had then migrated to southern Mesopotamia, where they probably subjugated a peasant population. During the fourth millennium a dozen or more Sumerian cities grew up in the lower Euphrates and Tigris valleys, each of them built around the shrine of a god, while in the fields outside peasants grew corn and date palms and herded cattle. One of the cities usually exercised hegemony over the others; but they remained largely independent in their internal affairs, and changes of supremacy were not infrequent. Sumerian civilization was based on the city-state and proved, in the end, unable to achieve integration on a larger scale. Entrusted by the gods with the management of their property, the priests and officials supervised agriculture on the temple estates and the building and repair of the irrigation canals, promoted trade and craftsmanship, and accumulated wealth; and the temples developed into elaborate financial institutions as well as places of worship and centers of learning. Below this ruling class was a body of free citizens, engaged in industry or cultivating farms, while the base of the social structure consisted of slaves recruited from prisoners of war or from citizens who had lost their freedom through inability to pay debts. Sumerian civilization became predominantly business-minded, and its development was accompanied by a considerable growth of trade both between different cities and with foreign peoples, the metals used by Sumerian craftsmen being imported from Anatolia and Iran and even as far as India.

The Sumerians never forgot that they had created their own means of support by building dry land in what had originally been a watery morass and confining the flood water in canals. This primal struggle with nature and the need for its constant renewal were central in their view of life. According to their mythology, the world had at first consisted of a watery chaos, and order had been established through a cosmic battle in which the gods had vanquished the forces of evil. This battle had to be repeated every spring, not only realistically by repairing the canals and keeping the rising waters under control, but also in symbolic rituals based on imitative magic, which served the purpose of unifying the community under theocratic leadership and concentrating its energies on the labors needed for survival. The priest-king of each city played the role of a god, usually of Enlil, who was the second figure of the Sumerian pantheon, being the son of the sky god Anu, and represented various forms of natural power and energy. In this role the king performed ceremonies depicting the defeat of Tiamat, the demon of the ocean, and the other monsters who followed her leadership. "In these festivals, which were state festivals, the human state contributed to the control of nature, to the upholding of the orderly cosmos. In the rites men secured the revival of nature in the spring, won the cosmic battle against chaos, and created the orderly world each year anew."[1] In other festivals priest-kings also assumed the identity of the vegetation spirit Tammuz, although these fertility rituals, which may have been established among the peasants before the coming of the Sumerians, were not integrated with the worship of Anu and Enlil and did not become part of the official state religion. Enacting these divine roles in religious dramas, the king became closely associated with the gods and was sometimes regarded as of divine descent, though according to the official theology he was always subordinate to his divine master and could not expect immortality. In Babylon, for example, his status was symbolized in an annual ceremonial in which he was stripped of his royal insignia, smitten in the face by a priest, and made to prostrate himself before the image of the city

[1] H. Frankfort (ed.), *Intellectual Adventure of Ancient Man,* p. 199.

god Marduk and confess his devotion; then, reclothed as a king, he was brought out weeping to show himself to his subjects.

In spite of the irrigation achievements of the Sumerians, they never developed any real sense of security. The movements of the waters were always uncertain; floods were frequent, and the Euphrates periodically changed its course. Mesopotamia, moreover, was surrounded by warlike and nomadic neighbors and was in danger of being conquered if she lost the capacity for self-defense. Fear was therefore always a predominant note in Sumerian religion. The gods could not wholly be trusted, and the unseen world was also peopled by a multitude of demons whose hostility had constantly to be averted by magical rites. Medicine, for example, consisted largely of an elaborate system of devices for exorcising evil spirits. And as the Sumerians had no faith in immortality, their hopes being concentrated on prosperity in this life, they devoted an extraordinary amount of effort and ingenuity to attempts to foretell the future. Retaining the primitive sense of man's unity with nature, and regarding the world as a god-created cosmic order, the order of human society being a reflection and imitation of the macrocosm, they supposed that all kinds of complex interrelationships could be discovered by careful observation. The priests therefore set out to trace correlations between human affairs and natural phenomena in an effort to find foreshadowings of impending catastrophes and thus enable men to guard themselves against coming misfortunes. Their favorite method of divination was to examine the livers of the animals sacrificed to the gods—a practice that spread to other parts of the Near East and was subsequently carried by the Etruscans to Italy and transmitted to the Romans. They also believed that they could foretell events by watching the movements of the stars. The study of astrology originated in the cities of early Mesopotamia, was further developed by the Chaldeans, who took possession of the city of Babylon in the first millennium B.C., and was afterwards transmitted to all parts of the civilized world.[2]

In spite of these irrational elements in their view of life, the Sumerians probably made more important contributions to man's cultural heritage than any other people known to history. They apparently invented writing, although they did not develop a phonetic

[2] In 1958 ten astrologers were listed in the Manhattan telephone book.

alphabet and were also handicapped by the necessity of using bulky clay tablets. Writing was used not only for religious and mythological poems and official records, but also for codes of law. The growth of commerce and moneylending led to an emphasis on contractual relationships, and this resulted in the formulation of the world's first legal systems. Sumerian craftsmen worked with soft metals as well as with stone, producing utensils, ornaments, and statues of gods and kings with an extraordinary grace and delicacy, in addition to inventing such objects as the socketed ax and the potter's wheel. In architecture, their most conspicuous creations were the immense brick ziggurats that inspired the story of the Tower of Babel; these were presumably erected in order that their gods might have habitations resembling the mountains from which they had originally come. But they also understood how to build arches and vaults, although these forms of construction do not seem to have been widely used, their importance not being recognized until they were adopted by the Romans more than three thousand years later. The most remarkable achievements of the Sumerians, however, were in astronomy and, more particularly, in mathematics. Notwithstanding their lack of an adequate system of notation, they developed not only arithmetic but also algebra, formulating certain algebraic methods of calculation which they were unable to transmit to their successors and which were rediscovered anew in very recent times.[3]

The Sumerian golden age apparently reached its peak before the end of the fourth millennium. The early centuries of the third millennium were largely filled with wars among the different cities, resulting in an increasing use of mercenary instead of citizen troops and in the militarization of society. Like the Greeks twenty-five hundred years later and the Italians forty-five hundred years later, the Sumerians, having achieved political integration on the basis of the city-state, were unable to make the necessary transfer of loyalties to any more comprehensive order. Meanwhile, predominance slowly passed to the Akkadians of northern Mesopotamia, a people who differed from the Sumerians in language and ethnic origin but who had largely been assimilated into Sumerian civilization. Halfway through the third millennium, Sargon, King of the Akkadian city of Agade, temporarily unified the whole of Mesopotamia in the world's first military empire.

[3] See George Sarton, *A History of Science,* pp. 68–74.

A few centuries later, supremacy was briefly recaptured by the Sumerian city of Ur, but through the following millennium Mesopotamia was ruled either by the Akkadians or by foreign conquerors, and eventually the Sumerians ceased even to speak their own language. The culture of Mesopotamia, however, was always based on its Sumerian foundation, to which other peoples added remarkably little, and the Sumerian language, although no longer spoken, continued to be studied (like Latin in medieval Europe) as the vehicle of learning. The economic and cultural traditions established by the Sumerians were, in fact, maintained in some form in the Mesopotamian cities for more than four thousand years, and the continuity was not finally broken until the region reverted to its primeval condition of watery chaos as a result of the destruction of the irrigation canals during the Mongol invasion of the thirteenth century of our era.

The civilization of Egypt, according to archaeological findings, first took shape under the stimulus of commercial contacts with the Sumerians, although after initial borrowings it quickly acquired its own distinctive quality. Human life was possible only close to the Nile, which flowed through a narrow valley for five hundred miles below the first cataract and then broadened into the delta before reaching the Mediterranean; and the dependence of the whole region on the annual flooding of the river made political unification essential. In prehistoric times a line of peasant communities grew up along the Nile valley. These "nomes" were afterwards combined into the two kingdoms of Upper and Lower Egypt, and finally, probably near the end of the fourth millennium, the whole country was united under a single ruler. The Egyptian Old Kingdom, which was the golden age of Egyptian civilization, lasted through most of the third millennium.[4]

The Egyptian mind was always dominated by an awareness of man's reliance upon natural regularities—the annual rise and fall of the river, the daily transit of the sun across the cloudless sky, and the abrupt division between the desert and the fertile fields of the Nile valley. Egypt, moreover, being bounded by the sea and the desert, was through much of its history almost isolated from the rest of the world and in little danger of foreign conquest; in spite of her

[4] The chronology of the early Egyptian dynasties was for a long time a controversial question; while a majority of Egyptologists dated the Old Kingdom in the third millennium, some scholars preferred to place it about one thousand years earlier. The question seems to have been finally settled in favor of the third millennium by the new methods of dating developed by the physicists.

early contacts with the Sumerians, which are known only through archaeology and were apparently forgotten by the Egyptians themselves, and in spite also of later trade relations with Phoenicia and some other areas, foreign peoples never had much reality in the Egyptian view of life. These conditions produced a civilization marked by its extraordinary sense of security and self-assurance and by its attempt to obliterate time and change. Content with their way of life and confident that it would never be disrupted by any accidental or unforeseen catastrophe, the early Egyptians believed that they could perpetuate it through all eternity; and while their primary aim was to transcend mortality by prolonging life beyond the grave, they did in fact succeed in maintaining their institutions for a longer period than any other people in history. Egyptian civilization has always fascinated mankind because of its sheer longevity. In the classical age of Greece the pyramids were already more than two thousand years old—a span almost as long as that separating the Greeks from ourselves—yet Egyptian society throughout this immense period had undergone only minor changes.

Before the unification of Egypt the different nomes worshipped their own tutelary gods, who seem to have originated as totem animals; and under the pharaohs these were combined into a single pantheon. Egyptian theology always remained an extraordinary tangle of deities with indeterminate personalities and overlapping functions, many of whom retained animal shapes and were believed to manifest themselves as bulls or birds. But the unifying religion of the pharaohs and the priests who supported them consisted chiefly of sun-worship. Each successive ruler was supposed to be the child of the sun god Re, who assumed human form for the purpose of begetting an heir to the throne. During the early dynasties he was also a falcon, this being apparently the totem of the nome whose ruler had first united the country. The most popular of Egyptian cults, however, was that of Osiris, the vegetation spirit who had been killed and then acquired immortality as ruler of the dead. In addition to being worshipped as the son of Re, the pharaoh also became identified with Horus, the son of Isis and Osiris, and ultimately with Osiris himself. The deification of the pharaoh was the essential bond of unity of the Egyptian state. The center of all the life of the community and the guardian and symbol of all natural and social order, he was responsible for performing the rituals that ensured that the sun and the river would continue their accustomed movements and for maintaining the irrigation canals and seeing that all classes of Egyptians attended to their prescribed duties.

In the Egypt of the Old Kingdom the pharaoh alone could be a complete individual, though his freedom was narrowly restricted by ritualistic requirements. The chief mark of his individuality was that he, and he alone, had the privilege of assured survival after death. During the early dynasties of the third millennium, a vast proportion of the economic resources of the state was devoted to ensuring that the pharaohs would enjoy their immortality under favorable conditions; human labor on an immense scale was conscripted for building the pyramids where they were buried, while the walls of their tombs were decorated with realistic pictures of Egyptian life, apparently in the magical expectation that they could be surrounded by their accustomed pleasures in the world of the dead. The striving of the early Egyptians for eternity by no means reflected any pessimistic repudiation of the world and the flesh; as their art makes manifest, it was, on the contrary, precisely because of their appreciation of daily life that they were so intent on immortality. The next world was not a recompense for the frustrations of this one, but an eternal prolongation of it. If one can judge from the surviving literary records, the tone of Egyptian society under the Old Kingdom was worldly, materialistic, and optimistic. As all men were officially the slaves of the god-king, society was not yet rigidly stratified along class lines, and ambitious individuals of humble origin could rise to positions of wealth and power in the bureaucracy by displaying skill and prudence, and might even hope that the pharaoh would continue to make use of their services in the next life.

Developing their own system of writing, the Egyptians invented papyrus, which was immeasurably more convenient than the clay tablets used in Mesopotamia. Somewhat inferior to the Sumerians in mathematics and astronomy, and also in metallurgy, they surpassed them in medicine and some other sciences, although their knowledge was always mixed with magical beliefs and never infused with any clear understanding of natural causation. Their literature included not only religious myths and incantations and official records, but also collections of maxims instructing young men how to achieve worldly success and works of fiction displaying a capacity for sophisticated humor. But their finest achievements were in the visual arts, in which they developed styles clearly indicative of the spirit of their civilization.

The main impetus of the arts in Egypt was a determination to affirm the reality of the everlasting world of the gods. Artists created many forceful and vivid portrayals of ordinary human beings and scenes of daily life; but this kind of realism was usually applied only to men and women of the lower classes, with the magical purpose of projecting them into the afterlife for the service of their rulers. The effort toward transcendence was particularly exemplified in bas-reliefs of gods and rulers in which the more important figures were presented frontally and placed side by side without movement or three-dimensional perspective, and in colossal statues of pharaohs whose majestic and impassive features, immune to human suffering and doubt, displayed their immortal nature. The Egyptian sculptor usually presented the human form with arms at the sides, hands clenched, and the left foot forward, and gave it large eyes, broad shoulders, and a slim waist. The shape of the body, the tense positions of the arms and legs, and the solemnity of the features reflected that drive of the human will toward the mastery of the natural world which characterized Egyptian civilization in all its aspects. Though never departing far from realistic representation, these sculptures sought constantly to deny change and movement and to distill out of natural appearances the forms that would be appropriate to eternity.[5] In architecture the Old Kingdom actually came as close to conquering time as is possible for any human enterprise. The Great Pyramid, built of more than two million blocks of limestone each averaging over two tons in weight, which were set in position and bound together with a geometrical accuracy and a thoroughness that modern engineering could hardly surpass, may well outlast the human race.

During the next two thousand years, Egypt passed through several periods of disintegration in which the monarchy was no longer strong

---

[5] While religious views of life have found their most typical expression in a purely abstract art, they have also been reflected in the treatment of the human figure. A society that affirms a belief in spiritual realities transcending sensuous experience is likely to produce an art in which figures are presented frontally, not in profile, and without movement or three-dimensional perspective. Human forms depicted in this manner give the impression of being removed from the world of space and time and engaged in the contemplation of eternal verities. Throughout art history frontality, immobility, and a restriction to two dimensions have been consistent indicators of a religious view of life. In the history of the Western world this was most clearly exemplified in late Roman and early Byzantine art.

The whole subject is explored by Arnold Hauser in his *Social History of Art.*

enough to maintain order, and power was assumed by local officials, and several times the country was reunited by new lines of pharaohs. But the mold set so firmly during the early dynasties was never broken; and in spite of a growing emphasis on military force, the development of private ownership of land by priests and nobles, and the gradual democratization of immortality, which finally became the goal of every Egyptian, the priestly castes of the temples always maintained the theocratic tradition. Relatively little was added to the science and culture of the Old Kingdom, styles of art and architecture continued almost unchanged, and the service of the god-king remained the essential unifying principle of Egyptian society.[6]

[6] By the sixteenth century of our era, the more advanced American Indian civilizations had reached a stage of development roughly comparable to that of Mesopotamia and Egypt during the theocratic period, and the descriptions written by their European conquerors illuminate the nature of theocratic society in general. By an interesting coincidence, the temple cities of the Mayas in southern Mexico, with their sacred pyramids, their astronomical studies, and their lack of unified government, seem remarkably like those of the early Sumerians, while the authoritarian state socialism of Inca Peru, governed by the children of the sun, strongly resembled that of early Egypt. In the first urban societies of America, as in those of the Old World, order and a sense of security were purchased by the surrender of responsibility to a theocratic ruling class. The weakness inherent in all such systems was vividly exemplified during the Spanish conquest. In Peru a mere handful of adventurers was able to secure mastery over millions of Indians simply by capturing the person of the Inca, thereby paralyzing the nerve center of the whole empire. A similar phenomenon probably occurred several times in the history of the ancient Near East.

IV CIVILIZATION: A RADIANT LIGHT?

Lewis Mumford

CIVILIZATION: AN AFFRONT TO HUMAN DIGNITY

Author of over twenty major books, lecturer, playwrite, and contributing editor to the New Republic for thirteen years, Lewis Mumford affords one of the more unique views on civilization. A mordacious critic of the dehumanizing tendencies of modern technology on civilization, Mumford transposes his thoughts to the dawn of civilization to demonstrate that technological advancement has always had its adverse effect on society. In contrast to the previous selections, which stress the advantages gained by man with the rise of civilization, Mumford seeks to show that, in some respects, civilization can be viewed as one long affront to human dignity.

At a late moment in man's emergence, he left behind the securities and intimacies and solidarities of tribal existence: what remained of archaic society served as the roadbed and right of way for the more mobile forms of civilization. At this point an audacious minority, in a handful of specially situated communities, made a daring thrust in a new direction: the experiment of civilization. With that step, the past ceases to be represented by dim campsites and scattered implements. We find buried cities, temples, all manner of works of art: presently, we come upon hieroglyphs and well-preserved records. But though all these data tell us much about what happened between the fourth millennium before Christ and the first, they do not tell why it happened. Here again we must fashion a myth to make the whole process a little more intelligible. . . .

How then did civilization come about? What process brought scores and hundreds of dispersed villages together into the political organization we now call the state? How did some of these villages increase in size and social complexity till they became a new kind of human settlement, the city, with its mixture of breeds, talents, and occupations, its divisions of labor, its variety of choices and its striking aesthetic forms? By what inner change did immemorial custom become written law, did the old village rituals become drama, and

From pp. 42, 44–70 in *The Transformations of Man* by Lewis Mumford, in Volume Seven of World Perspectives Series, Planned and Edited by Ruth Nanda Anshen. Copyright © 1956 by Lewis Mumford. Used by permission of Harper & Row, Publishers, Inc. and by permission of George Allen & Unwin Ltd.

magical practices turn into an organized and unified religious cult, built upon cosmic myths that open up vast perspectives of time, space, power? Why, in short, has a growing portion of mankind, for the last four or five thousand years, committed itself to civilization—or, like folk society, let itself be drawn along in its wake?

Properly, we reject the eighteenth-century myth of the social contract, in which each member of the community gave up his original autonomy and freedom for the overall protection of life and property that came with organized government. But at the core of this myth lies a kernel of truth: the institutions of civilization were the outcome of deliberate invention and conscious choice: indeed, they seem part of a general growth of self-consciousness, individual and collective. Behind them is no mere automatic accretion, but a mighty effort of collective will. With this new consciousness went something that seems relatively absent from the stable, well-integrated culture of simpler societies: internal struggle, competition, tension, conflict.

Civilization brought a new kind of unity based on division and specialization: a new uniformity imposed by deliberate repression: a new agreement that sprang out of a partial reconciliation of opposites, not, as in primitive society, out of ancestral unanimity, born of a common understanding as to the ultimate nature and purpose of life. If archaic culture rests on an internalized law and order, hardly ever consciously formulated, civilization rests on an externalized law and order, more far-reaching than man had ever established before, binding together with explicit rules and regulations dissimilar communities and varied local customs.

Economically, the new order was based largely on the forcible exploitation of cultivators and artisans by an armed and ever-threatening minority: mobile intruders or heavily entrenched lords of the land. For civilization brought about the equation of human life with property and power; indeed, property and power became more dear than life. Labor ceased to be a shared communal function: it became degraded into a purchasable commodity, bought and sold in the marketplace: even sexual "service" could be bought. This systematic subordination of life to its mechanical and legal agents existed at the beginning of civilization and still haunts every existing society; at bottom, the goods of civilization have been achieved and preserved—and this is a crowning contradiction—largely by methodical compulsion and regimentation, backed by a flourish of force. In that sense, civilization is one long affront to human dignity.

The general conditions for this transformation have now become fairly clear, though the details differ widely from region to region. Between 7000 and 2000 B.C. a series of great technical advances were made on a wide front, from Egypt to China: beginning with the domestication of plants, and furthered by the taming of cattle and beasts of burden. Above all, the cultivation of the hard grains, on fertile irrigable land, made it possible to nourish large populations in a small territory: these crops, which could be held over from the fat years to the lean years, produced security and continuity and settlement on a scale that had never been possible before. The bronze age, with its costly weapons and chariots, which gave a monopoly of power to their possessors, furthered centralized political control; while the succeeding iron age cheapened all the new facilities for conquering nature and enslaving men.

Once the ox and the plow were introduced, the rich heavy soils of the river valleys, the most open routes of communication and transport, could be cultivated. With a large supply of surplus labor available, the swift technical advances in water control—canals, irrigation, ditches, embankments, even the turning of the course of rivers, as in Mesopotamia—became possible. With these collective improvements the whole river valley became an economic and political unit. These physical changes were accompanied by comparable political and social inventions: for civilization brought about a double transformation of man. On one hand it developed in the pharaoh or ruler, the autonomous personality; and on the other, by the subdivision of labor and the specialization of work, it produced the submissive, if not servile *Teilmensch,* or divided man, who has lost his primitive wholeness without yet gaining the new attribute of his ruler: autonomy.

Let us deal with the second transformation first. In the simple structure of primitive society, roles and occupational activities were largely interchangeable: apart from the biological specialization of sex, each member, in the appropriate situation, could play any role that any other member could play. As the cycle of the year revolved, as the phases of life unfolded, so did the works and duties of the members of the community. The fact that one did a job well did not condemn one to performing it for a whole lifetime, except perhaps in the earliest type of specialist, the shaman or priest.

Civilization, in contrast, created occupational groups with permanent fixed roles: soldiers, merchants, scholars, scribes, administrators. In numbers that no earlier culture could have supported, these specialized groups practiced their callings, with mechanical efficiency and *expertise*. From now on, right down to our own day, *"life"* means essentially working life, withdrawn from the general interests of the rural household—especially for the male members of the urban community. Though until modern times these specialized callings probably never constituted more than a small fraction of the total population—at most possibly 10 percent—their specialized efficiency and their conscientious dedication to work set the mode for "civilized" life. The gods themselves reflected the principle of specialization: each had his prescribed sphere and role, but none, not even Atum or Marduk, exercised all the functions of deity.

By thus building a corporate society, composed of a multitude of castes, professions, guilds, associations, civilized man lost the neighborly unison of the village community, in which work and play and family and religion were closely intermingled: above all he lost its single-mindedness. But he gained detachment and diversity; and the partial selves that he created revealed, long before he invented specialized machines, the possibilities of a limited mechanical order. Traditionally it takes nine tailors to make a man: but Charles Fourier[1] was not far from wrong when he declared that it took 1,760 partial men (specialists) to make a man. But it is only in the mind that such a gargantuan creature could exist.

Each civilized group cultivated interests, routines, "mysteries," which kept it from identifying its life with that of the whole society. The very fact that this complex society was no longer the visible community of the village encouraged a certain degree of withdrawal and disaffection. In the act of entering their special association, its members left behind—and indeed deliberately excluded—other rival organs. Each occupation had its rites of initiation and its professional secrets. At its highest levels, it operated as a conspiracy to preempt for the smaller group an undue share of the goods of the larger community. The social division of classes, based on private property,

---

[1] Charles Fourier (1772–1837) was a French Utopian Socialist.—Ed.

and the economic division of occupations, based on technical specialization, thus tended to work toward the same general result: they erected a partial self that put its own specialized competence above the whole self, and a partial community (the "insiders") that placed its own advantage above that of the whole community.

At first the gain to the prospering individual seemed indisputable. Civilized man, at an early stage, achieved a degree of autonomy, independence, self-consciousness—and therewith choice—that was unknown in primitive society. Each of the heroes in the *Iliad* was a highly individualized character in his own right, not just an undifferentiated Greek or Trojan. But as the outcome of this process, civilized man became, as we say, selfish: he no longer identified his personal concerns with the health and the prosperity of the group. In sinking into a bigger community whose membership he could never know intimately or even fully conceive in its concrete variety, civilized man took advantage of this relative anonymity. He was tempted to appropriate for himself what once belonged to the entire society. "I and mine" now counted for more than "We and ours." Where the standards of civilization remain uppermost, these generalizations still hold.

The other transformation of civilized man moved precisely in the opposite direction: toward the elevation of a unique personality, possessing powers uncircumscribed by the usages of society. This change at first came about through the very complexity of the new river civilizations, with their need to control the flow of water, to mark boundaries when effaced by flood, to impose communal labor and to collect taxes, to supervise trade, codify laws, guard frontiers. In this new order, the capital city was the social agent of unification; and within that city, the palace and temple were the seats of concentrated power and bureaucratic administration. Within the palace and temple one figure stood supreme: the deified ruler. In him alone man first achieved individuality.

At the top of the political and social pyramid towered the absolute monarch. He replaced the archaic council of elders, the local assembly of free—but custom-bound—men. This elevation of a single ruler took place, Henri Frankfort[2] has told us, in times of emer-

---

[2] Henri Frankfort (1897–1954) was Professor of Oriental Archaeology at the University of Chicago for seventeen years. In 1949 he was appointed Director of the

gency, when quick decisions had to be made. The king alone, by literally personifying society, could escape from the fetters of local custom and routine, or proverbial wisdom that no longer was in touch with new realities. The royal fiat gave to the actions of society, too long fettered by precedent and collective inertia, the attributes of an integrated person: freedom, the power of detached judgment and intelligent choice, a swift, unified response. Herodotus[3] long ago made the same observation: picturing the lawlessness and confusion among the Medes, he told how Deioces, a man of mark in his own village, rose to supreme rulership by applying himself to the practice of justice. Such a concentration of power and responsibility must have occurred in many areas, as society became more complex and unexpected crises called for new measures. At such moments the decisive change from a dispersed village culture to centralized urban control probably took place—though historically it often relapsed, under pressure, into a more localized feudal kind of authority.

But the point to note is that, in both government and religion, the absolute ruler first developed an autonomous personality, completely detached from its social envelope: for both good and bad a law unto himself. While the subdivision of labor diffused itself rapidly through society, the development of the complete autonomous person has remained a rare occurrence throughout human history. If at a relatively early date the common man shared his divine ruler's claims to immortality, it is only after thousands of years that other attributes of royalty have been, reluctantly and grudgingly, passed on to the community as a whole, and treated as a natural attribute of man.

The prime mark of civilization, then, is the bringing together of larger bodies of men, by means of technical agents, symbolic abstractions, and centralized political authority, into a greater community of purpose than had ever existed before. Written records and the practice of recordkeeping, written legends and myths, the common calendar, the common monetary unit, the common law, the common utilities, the common meeting place, capable of uniting tens of thousands of people into a cohesive organization, were all immense

---

Warburg Institute and Professor of the History of Pre-classical Antiquity in the University of London. His extensive fieldwork in Iraq produced much new information on the early history of Babylonia.—Ed.

[3] Herodotus (c. 489–420 B.C.) was an early Greek historian from Halicarnassus in Asia Minor. His work, the first comprehensive attempt at secular narrative history, earned for him the title "father of history."—Ed.

achievements. By these agents of a common order and a common life mankind still continues to live. Insofar as it has made possible this enlargement of the human circle, civilization justifies, in no little measure, its heavy exactions.

But unfortunately this transformation of man has an ugly side: civilized man, if more law-abiding, is likewise more calculating: if he is more skillful and intelligent, he is more selfish. If he is stirred by ambitions and desires that were foreign to the modest expectations of archaic culture, he is also subject to perverse derangements and criminal insubordinations: as a result, civilization has often brought about gigantic miscarriages of life, in bestialities and butcheries that simpler communities lack the animus as well as the power to inflict.

Something intimate and indubitably precious was lost in the transition to civilization, or almost lost. But the decrease in depth was partly offset by a gain in breadth: under the rule of a common law and a common way of life, a much larger body of people met and mingled. Civilization at least overcame the insularity and isolation of primitive rural society.

For all its internal contradictions, the development of civilization brought real goods no primitive society could show. By the sheer weight of numbers, civilization gave its members new social and intellectual advantages. If there is likely to be one person of exceptional ability in every generation, in say ten thousand people, a group of only a thousand people may have to wait many generations before it has the advantage of a superior mind; and that mind, by its very isolation, may find nothing to nourish it. But a hundred thousand people, in Sumer or Akkad, in Athens or Rome, in Peking or Benares, might produce at least fifty good minds in a single lifetime; and these minds, by the very fact of close communication in space and time, would be open to a variety of challenges and stimuli not possible if they appeared alone. So, too, specialization in trades and occupations, and further refinement of skills, depend upon mere numbers, both to provide the demand and produce the necessary variety of services. Once these conditions obtain, greater productivity will follow, even without mechanical invention.

With exemplary symbolism, the function of the Egyptian creator god, Atum, "was to bring the world into order and assign places and functions." There lay the achievement of civilization: it multiplied power and widened order: visible power in armies and work gangs, visible order in canals, storehouses, cities. The beauty of an ordered life was no small aesthetic triumph. But in this achievement, the repetitive-compulsive note was never entirely absent: regularity, formal discipline, specialized efficiency were purchased only by a willingness to exclude many of the tempting departures that life may spontaneously offer. The holiday functions of life themselves became segregated and specialized, as erotic expression itself did, in the interests of working efficiency and order. That pervasive order has stamped the "civilized self."

Though the whole routine of life became more elaborate, civilization, by its mastery of physical organization, liberated whole classes from the necessity of breadwinning and permitted them to cultivate their minds, likewise in an orderly fashion. In the city, the economic surplus was funneled into capital investments no mere primitive culture could afford: temples, palaces, observatories, libraries, courts of justice, came into existence, along with the daily activities that went on within them. If often misused, these institutions ultimately served all men. In the dynamic interplay of social and personal functions life itself became a drama, and the drama in time typified and reflected life. Civilized man, indeed, was "not himself" outside the city; for without this urban background he faltered in the interpretation of his roles and missed his cues.

In Chaldea and Egypt, the priesthood extended their special power and authority through observation of the skies: they studied the passage of the heavenly bodies and established the solar year. This astronomical measurement brought regularity into life: personal order conformed in some measure to this impersonal (cosmic) order. By synchronizing the actions of men with predictable natural cycles and recurrent events, the calendar eventually introduced a seasonable sequence into all activities, beginning with agriculture. In turn, the discipline of astronomy refined the whole process of calculating and counting: the abstractions of number made possible a new kind of symbolism that came in with civilization: the symbolism of money —and finally the equation of power and wealth with money.

Civilization replaced a primitive life economy with a money economy, at least in the great urban centers: though the archaic life economy kept a hold over the rural areas, only slightly corroded by the abstract love of gain. In the new urban environment, civilized man was stirred by ambitions and emulations, by anxieties and imaginative projections that man did not know in the archaic period: the voice of Hesiod or Amos, speaking on behalf of archaic man, rose in anxious protest against this new conception of human life. They had reason for this protest. There was doubtless a certain intensification of life in the great urban centers, among those who had mastered the new procedures of religion and trade and law and administration: but there was also—then as now—a falling off of life, a lowering of values, in the small tributary communities. As society as a whole became more powerful, through organization, discipline, coordination, division of labor, each individual person became enfeebled: he was reduced to a fractional part, and no longer exercised either the understanding or control that was his in a small community: he had become a vicarious participator in the values of the great community. Certainly, the corporate power of civilization was much greater than man could achieve within the more personal sphere of the village community: was this, perhaps, why he came to value, indeed to worship, his corporate self, in the person of the monarch, as the highest possible good: no less than a god? Both in origin and in modern times, that corporate projection seems to be a compensation for the meagerness of personal existence.

Some of civilization's imputed benefits may have been challenged by archaic man; he might well have anticipated the disaffected sailor in Melville's *Redburn*,[4] who felt that the only result of "snivelization" was to make men snivel. Looking back over the whole development, one may still challenge some of the institutions that have been most rigidly structured into every civilization, without, like Rousseau, also rejecting the goods that were in fact promoted.

Note the social contradiction. For those who mastered the arts of civilization, it brought, no doubt, an intensification of life, a heightening of consciousness, a sense of the individual ego combined with a pride in collective achievement that justified the sacrifice it demanded. But those upon whom the sacrifices were imposed formed a majority of the population, and their willingness to submit to this compulsive routine remains, even now, a little mysterious. For one thing, the division of labor closed many doors that were open in a more loosely organized society; and the habit of working day after

---

[4] Herman Melville's well-known nautical novel, *Redburn* (1849).—Ed.

day at the same task, without any immediate reward, deferring present goods for doubtful future benefits, with the work life itself absorbing energy that might be profitably expended in the offices of love and parenthood—all this is not self-explanatory, still less self-justifying. Though one must allow for the pride and presumption of the scribe, who put his own profession above all others, the early Egyptian *Satire on the Trades* (*circa* 2000 B.C.) utters a judgment on this general depletion of life that remains classic. Yet from the beginning civilization rested on the depersonalization of mechanized effort; and cheerful submission to this routine is perhaps the chief mark of civilized man. If no external master exercises this authority, civilized man will impose the pattern on himself, in pursuit of money, prestige, or power.

The repression that Sigmund Freud regarded as a necessary accompaniment of civilization is indeed a fact: but it is not confined to sexual activities. Rather, it applies to all the autonomous functions, and still more to autonomous expressions. Sex itself has rather a compensatory role: from the orgiastic rituals of early religions to the exploitation of sex for political and commercial purposes in later societies, sexuality serves as counter-weight to other forms of denial. Woman, in pursuit of her own biological goals, has always been in some measure opposed to this narrowing scheme of life: in that sense, Meredith's[5] dictum that woman would be the last creature to be civilized by man is profoundly true. When in modern times women claimed the right to take part in all the occupations men practiced, they forgot to ask how far these occupations were self-justifying, or what modifications might be made in their compulsive rituals to fit them more closely to the central needs of life. Instead of restoring men to a whole life that fully included woman's own special interests, love, sex, human nurture, the leaders of feminism were too easily content with the half-life men had allotted to themselves.

While the working life of civilized man is itself something of an aberration, in the unconditional submission it exacts, its ambivalent achievements in law and order seem even more open to criticism. By organizing the police functions of the state, civilized man increased the internal security of its members, rescuing them from blood feuds, random violence, and unjust deprivation of freedom or

[5] Reference here is to the English novelist and poet George Meredith (1828–1909). —Ed.

property. But the price of peace and security and justice within the state was an extension of insecurity and violence outside the domestic realm.

From the beginning, as Plato long ago observed, war was the natural relation of civilized states to one another. The ultimate irrationality of civilization was to invent, perfect, and incorporate into the whole structure of civilized life the art of war. For war was not a mere residue of more common primitive forms of aggression, as depicted in the myth of Leviathan. In all its typical aspects, its discipline, its drill, its handling of large masses of men as units, in its destructive assaults *en masse,* in its heroic sacrifices, its final destructions, exterminations, seizures, enslavements, war was rather the special invention of civilization: its ultimate drama. The final negation that tragically justified all its preparatory negations. The organized army was not merely the instrument but the symbol of civilized power—the first application of technology to politics. Like the genocidal applications of nuclear energy in our time, it effectively undermined the creative achievements of civilization.

Apart from its more obvious pretexts, the expansion of state power and the seizure of manpower, the possibility of gaining by pillage more than can be won in a short time by toil, war had still another reason for existence: it projected outside the state the internal conflicts that civilization at once promoted and drastically repressed within the state. While every civilization released opportunities for human development that were not possible till large groups of men were welded together into great intercommunicating organizations, it likewise compounded explosive forces that repeatedly got beyond control. If organized force brings civilizations into existence, organized force is likewise the agent of disintegration that ultimately brings them to an end.

Aside from playing this sinister part, the institution of war had other unfavorable effects in curtailing the benefits of civilization: for in time it brought a habit of regimentation into activities that might, under the influence of more healthy human needs, have liberated themselves from routine. Under the general pressure of drill, sharpened by vocational specialization, civilized man turned himself into a mechanical object, long before he invented any comparable complex and effective nonhuman mechanism. With the development of civilization, its useful divisions of labor—not necessarily harmful, if kept open and interchangeable—hardened into rigid caste systems. This tendency was pushed to its logical conclusion in the hereditary social castes of India, in turn minutely divided into occupational castes, but no civilization has been free from this kind of caricature of the figure of man. Men made themselves into collective machines thousands of years before they acquired sufficient technical skill to make machines into working counterparts of their collective selves.

Though no human group has yet gone so far as to make the worker caste unfit for reproduction, the actual physiological differences between classes and occupations still leaves a marked trail over their disease and death rate even in progressive countries; and even in relatively dynamic societies, caste lines and relatively small economic and social differences may not be passed over easily: status is often more important than functional capacity.

Thus man, in achieving the docilities and cooperation of civilization, independently reinvented an institution not found in nature except among creatures who are equally divided and crippled in their nature: the social insects. Now that he must undo this radical error, in order to save himself from his own misguided inventions, it is time to reexamine with a sharper eye other related institutions he has taken too complacently for granted.

Slavery, compulsory labor, social regimentation, economic exploitation, and organized warfare: this is the darker side of the "progress of civilization." In modified forms, these negations and repressions are still active today; indeed, while part of the curse of forced labor has been lifted, through the invention of power-driven and automatic machinery, war has taken on an infinitely more destructive form: breaking through all physical barriers and moral restraints, it has turned in our own day into unrestricted genocide, which now threatens all life on this planet.

This was a heavy price to pay for the humanizing feats of civilization: yet all over the world men once paid that price. Though from the very beginning a dominant minority took command of the agents of civilization and appropriated its goods, the mass of mankind tamely acquiesced in that act.

This whole perversion of the universal goods of civilization to the interests of a few seems to defy reason and baffle explanation. By what process did the mass of men come to accept it so meekly?

The disciplinary rigors, the systematic sacrifices, might all be justi-fied on a shrewd balance of gains and losses, if the resultant goods were evenly distributed over the whole society. But for thousands of years nothing like such a distribution was even thought of, much less attempted. It was only grudgingly that the principle of justice was applied even to particular wrongs, so that the judge would give the verdict, not to those who had bribed him most heavily, but to him who was entitled to it by right: it was a milestone in justice, as Breasted[6] has pointed out, when a judge went so far as to decide a case at law against his own relatives. Slaves and poor men had no rights that their superiors would recognize; and they gain a foothold on the social ladder in one era only to lose it again.

The reason for civilization's acceptance remains undiscoverable until we allow for the influence of the irrational and the supernatural. Civilization was made possible by an inner transformation almost too deep for analysis: a transformation that brought into existence two magnified kinds of being, the hero and the god, and combined their functions in the office of kingship. In this change civilized man freed himself partly from his preoccupation with his inner self: he turned increasingly to external objects, detached from bodily feel-ings: his ideal self was the hero, the person of giant strength, capable of performing mighty feats of prowess, like the labors of Heracles, and his hero god was a Prometheus, who stole fire from heaven for the benefit of man.

The trials that the hero faces are physical trials: the slaying of giants and dragons, the moving of giant stones, the turning of the course of rivers; and it was in such feats that the godlike monarchs of ancient civilizations traditionally excelled. Such a turning toward outward reality may be a historic sign of the integration of the human ego: a prime acknowledgment of everything outside the self that re-sists it and independently reacts on it. This was the way to further individuation and conscious control over both the outer and the in-ner world. Certainly the epics of the heroes seem to flourish precisely at this moment of emergence; and in that general change of con-sciousness even those who were deprived and oppressed have shared—as the exploited factory workers of the nineteenth century shared the belief in mechanical improvement and social progress.

6 James Henry Breasted (1865–1935), who established the study of Egyptology in the United States and became the foremost authority in this field.—Ed.

Through the hero and the king, man achieved a more exalted image of himself: a sense of capabilities for action and achievement that he had hardly dreamed of before. We may infer from the appearance of winged creatures in art that the audacious dream of human flight itself took shape at this moment: there is no evidence of it in the representations of the palaeolithic cave man. In the person of the hero, civilized man imposed on himself heavier tasks, demanding longer periods of concentrated effort, than he had ever before undertaken. Relaxation and indulgence, the normal rewards of normal toil, now seemed to him perils rather than attractions. Gilgamesh, in the early Babylonian epic, rejected the love of the goddess, Inanna, but readily slew the bull she sent against him. Odysseus, under Calypso's enchantment, lost his initiative; and Samson, by sinking into the arms of Delilah, was shorn of his physical power. Only by spurning his sexuality, pouring all his energies into work, will the hero have the power to perform these superhuman tasks. The pioneers of civilization are not at home in woman's world; on their typical adventures they leave her behind. If, like Heracles, they boast of having intercourse with fifty women in one night, that boast itself shows that they confused the mere breaking of records with amorous delight—a further proof of their undeveloped erotic life.

Primitive man was sustained by a sense of union with his world: stones, trees, animals, spirits, people, all spoke to him and responded to him; and he was in them and of them. Civilized man throve on struggle and opposition: he must master or be mastered, and the more formidable the struggle the greater his own sense of life. Dominated by this attitude he punishes himself, as well as those who are the objects of his aggression; and it is in the negative moments of life, in flood, shipwreck, earthquake, fire, or war, that he rises to his highest achievements, while periods of prosperity leave him fat and foolish, without a worthy object that evokes his extraverted powers.

With civilization, life became something more than a repetitive round of days and acts, however harmonious: it was an *agon,* or contest: a test of strength and skill, in which powers of endurance might be pushed to a heartbreaking point: literally an agony. By projecting the hero and emulating his acts, civilized man lengthened his span of attention and increased the pressure of effort. In his more anxious moments, he ensured beforehand the ability to perform superhuman feats by exercise, self-discipline, drill. But one cannot command these new powers without renunciation: a modicum of death is part of the daily routine: life postponed, life diminished, life denied. The fact is that civilization, for all its immense increase in vitality, casts contempt on the life-nurturing functions as weak, sentimental, effeminate. In civilized man, sexuality and work reverse their roles: production dominates reproduction, and field and womb alike take second place.

But if the hero symbolized the new processes of civilization, with their vehement dedication to work, it was through the cult of the gods, subjectively magnified, that civilized man evoked from his own unconscious the powers that helped offset the brutalities and deprivations of his new mode of life. For with civilization, his animal sources of vitality had been threatened, and his sense of resentment did not quickly disappear. A consciousness of the imminence of death haunts him, perhaps because the larger life civilization opens has quickened his expectations. Instead of taking death naturally, civilized man fights against it: indeed a good part of his life becomes a dramatization of this struggle. Sumerian mythology plainly indicates a conviction that the ruling cosmic powers had stacked the cards against man and that death always wins the game. But the Egyptians, through the very elaborateness of their counter-measures—the mummy, the tomb, the pyramid—almost deceived themselves into believing that they had transposed death into life. The ironic price of that triumph was to make death supreme in both realms.

Civilization accordingly expanded man's fears as well as his knowledge; and in turn the powers of the universe themselves loomed larger as his own corporate powers increased: so the gods became responsible for all the phenomena of earth and heaven, of life and death. Only by submission, indeed, blind obedience, could ordinary men hope to be the beneficiary of their powers. This sense of human inadequacy seems to have enlarged as the community itself, by its expansion and increasing complexity, grew beyond the human scale: even the absolute ruler became as circumscribed in his moves as is the king in the ancient game of chess—that admirable symbol of the chief agents and gambits of civilization.

As reason and order began methodically to prevail in life, the irrational and the supernatural intervened in order to maintain social stability; for religion, by commanding service to the gods, restored the capacity of a community to endure through the common efforts and sacrifices of its members, at the moment when selfish rationality would have counseled each member to seek only his private good in his own limited lifetime. When the conditions of daily living pressed hard, multiplying the frustrations and self-mutilations needed to keep the civilized order together, religion opened more distant prospects and a happier destination: another world and another life. Henri Bergson's[7] description of religion, as an offset to consciousness of the brevity of life, the certainty of death, and the disparity between our plans and our achievements, applies with particular force to the preaxial religions of early civilizations. But some of these preoccupations lingered in the higher religions that followed.

Civilization, then, provided the insurgent and irrational elements in man's nature with a vast imaginative outlet through highly institutionalized religion. Here civilized man confronted the many mysterious forces that sometimes seem to further his life, yet sometimes seem quite at cross-purposes with it; here, too, by transference and identification with deity, he added to his own sense of power. Yet the transposition of life into immortality, of human ignorance into divine omniscience, was not easily effected. At his first moment of relaxation, Gilgamesh lost the fruit that gave eternal life to the serpent, while merely eating of the fruit of the knowledge of good and evil brought Adam and Eve's exile from Paradise.

Religion, as it comes before us in the early civilizations, is plainly an upsurging of unconscious forces. These divine powers seem to erupt from the hot magma of the human soul: the gods at first have nothing to do with morality or civic duty, with love and justice. So far from being moralizers, the gods are rather pure expressions of lust, ferocity and wanton energy: the very qualities that civilization, seemingly for man's own good, seeks to modify and soften, or at least to divert to more pragmatic purposes. Listen to what Horus says to the enemies of his father, Osiris.[8] "Your arms are tied to your heads, O you evil ones. You are fettered from behind, you are the evil ones to be decapitated—you shall not exist." This same un-

---

[7] Henri Bergson (1859–1941), a noted French philosopher who won the 1927 Nobel Prize in literature for his philosophical works.—Ed.
[8] Mumford refers here to the Egyptian myth of how Horus, one of the great gods of Egypt, avenged the death of his father, Osiris, aided by his mother Isis.—Ed.

restrained murderous anger belches forth likewise from the mouth of Yahweh: he who unlooses every method of extermination, from sword to plague, upon those who stand in the way of his Chosen People.

One may interpret the insolent powers of these monstrous divinities, at least in part, as attempts to restore by unconscious projection the human vitalities repressed by civilization: they were likewise a means—irrational but plausible—of creating an active superpersonal authority to make up for the absence of an archaic morality based on consensus, in a mixed urban society filled with newcomers and outsiders who had few shared values and common folkways. Finally the gods, though created independently of this need, lent countenance to social stratifications that nullified the natural harmonies and human solidarities of more primitive cultures.

In time the unconscious processes that create divinities become subject to corruption by conscious manipulation. As early as the Egyptian *Book of the Dead,* we find the priesthood supplementing faith by magic and guaranteeing immortality at so much per head, in written documents that leave a blank space for the buyer to fill in: many thousands of years before Jacob Fugger, in the sixteenth century, purchased the exclusive agency for selling holy Christian indulgences. This goes along with the identification of supernatural religious power, plainly projected from man's unconscious, with organized political power, marshaled into action by the officers of the state, whose head may be a priest or even a god. The recurrence of these debasements in all religions justifies the cynical grin of Voltaire.

If, despite these crudities and perversions, religion has played an integral part in every civilization, it is because the mysterious forces discernible in both the cosmos and the human soul are too important to remain unacknowledged. Both for good and bad, religion magnified the realm of creative possibility. In religion, civilization compensated for its own frustrations by creating aesthetic objects and ideal presences, deeply rooted in man's nature, and so imposing that man became more deeply attached to them than to life itself.

As long as their faith in the gods and their expectations of a life to come remained active, that is, as long as they could draw on springs of life in their unconscious to offset the aridities and rigidities of civilization, the daily claims of the outer world could be met, with resignation if not with cheerfulness. What happens when the external exactions become heavier, and the unconscious itself becomes empty of everything except a turbid, poisonous residue of demonic life, we only now begin to realize in our own day. Such stability as civilizations achieved—and the civilization most completely dominated by other-worldly religion, Egypt, lasted the longest—was due to the fact that an uneasy balance between the inner and the outer state was effected.

In time, as man mastered the civil arts of cooperation, his gods became more tender and beneficent. Thanks to the transcendent claims of religion, civilization encouraged man's higher functions as never before. With power came leisure, with leisure came reflective thought. The physical exertions of the hunter and the miner and the peasant absorb all vitality in the daily round: Emerson's discovery, that a morning spent in gardening left him destitue of any ideas, bears a universal application. Too much physical exertion, like too much liquor, too heavy a meal, too much sexual intercourse, lessens the possibility of productive thought.

In setting aside a class that nourished the products of the unconscious, by solitary communion and orderly public ritual, religion likewise extended the province of conscious, directed thought: the priest, the prophet, the sage, the scholar, the scientist, the bard were all members of one family; and in time they gathered sufficient strength to break through both the compulsive routines of civilization and the compensating irrationalities of the early religions.

If our myth has accounted for the general acceptance of civilization, despite the fact that it gave so much to so few and so little to so many, we have still only partly explained its long dominance. We are left with the fact that each of the great civilizations has been self-limited and self-enclosed: so much so that in our time two voluminous philosophies of history have been written without their authors' taking into account the underlying extensions of communication and mutual aid which even the brutal conquests of an Alexander or a Genghis Khan in some degree served. Yet without constantly enlarging the boundaries of human intercourse, without making its powers more obedient to human intention, what justification can civilization offer for its curtailment of life's full possibilities? Are either the gods or the goals of civilization a worthy terminus for human effort?

The fact is that man has never wholeheartedly accepted civilization or loved his completely civilized self. Beneath class conflicts and rebellions against the unjust economic arrangements that so long remained engrained in civilization, one detects even more corrosive assaults, brought about by the beneficiaries of civilization, who cure their boredom in war and recover purpose by spreading destruction.

Civilization saved itself mainly through two devices: a constant recruitment of fresh, undisillusioned personnel, brought in every generation from the rural areas, still throbbing with unspoiled life; and, no less, a persistence of rural habits and customs, and an infiltration of homely wisdom, from one of the earliest of didactic writings, that of worldly-wise Ptah-Hotep in Egypt, to the parables of Jesus. In short, civilization, at least up to our own time, has always been sustained by pagan vitalities, undivided and undepressed; and when these ceased to be sufficient, it was redeemed again, as we shall see, by the opening up of a post-civilized prospect, through the agency of the axial religions, transposing all the values of civilization into a new mode of life, and so using even its worst features as a condition for salvation.

But note: the very extension of civilization weakened the fabric of archaic society, whose elementary morality sustained it: what men had once done unconsciously, for the good of their visible neighbor, they found it hard to do consciously, for the good of many invisible neighbors. It was not by accident that Augustus Caesar followed up the consolidation of the Roman Empire by attempting to revive the festivals and rituals of archaic society: he seems to have grasped intuitively that the vast mechanical fabric of Roman civilization was not self-sustaining, and he hoped, it seems, to cement it on the lower level of folk feeling and sexual renewal, if not on the upper level of conscious ethical purpose, as the Stoics had sought to do.

The heroic efforts that enabled men to take the great step toward mechanical organization and sustained common effort far beyond the immediate needs for survival eventually give way, in every civilization, to a dreary later stage, the unadventurous one of keeping the wheels turning. Then the will to order ceases to be self-sustain-

ing and inherently purposeful: life becomes empty. Are not the sacrifices and burdens greater than the tangible rewards? At a certain
stage of every civilization, accordingly, it reaches a point revealed
in the early Egyptian Dialogue Between Man and His Shadow Self,
or Soul, when he asks himself why he should go on living: would
he not be better dead? This internal dissolution of meaning and
value may be hastened by external mischances and failures, such
as Arnold Toynbee has examined in great detail; but as he wisely
points out, the main blows come from within. Perhaps the most serious limitation is that the effort to expand the physical shell of civilization—as the main source of its values—leads to a thickening of
its walls and a steadily diminishing amount of space for the living
creature within. Civilization begins by a magnificent materialization
of human purpose: it ends in a purposeless materialism. An empty
triumph, which revolts even the self that created it.

The sudden evaporation of meaning and value in a civilization,
often at the moment when it seems at its height, has long been one
of the enigmas of history: we face it again in our own time. If the
values of civilization were in fact a sufficient fulfillment of man's nature, it would be impossible to explain this inner emptiness and
purposelessness. Military defeats, economic crisis, political dissen-
sions, do not account for this inner collapse: at best they are symp-
tomatic, for the victor is equally the victim and he who becomes rich
feels impoverished. The deeper cause seems to be man's self-aliena-
tion from the sources of life.

When continued frustration and despair finally produce existential
nausea, only desperate courses seem to open. The mildest of these
courses is that of escapism: withdrawal from society by physical
adventure or by spiritual seclusion, often in the *sauve qui peut* mood
of the refugee, fleeing from disaster. Lacking this avenue, the old
anesthetics of strong drink and sexual promiscuity offer quick alle-
viation, only to deepen the original disgust that prompted their use.
Still another way, even more desperate and self-defeating, is to concentrate further on the technical agents that have made life so meaningless, making the machine a fetish that serves as an object of love,
otherwise thwarted. Too often this technical glorification carries out
the most perverse infantile fantasies, and turns into a corrupt assault
on all that is still vital and healthy.

Against this chronic miscarriage of civilization the official religious cults offered no relief: indeed their own institutional paraphernalia, their own exorbitant material demands, only added to the economic burden without lifting the inner depression. Only one course has so far opened up the way to further development: one that challenges the axioms of civilization and places human life on a new foundation. This was originally the moment of the axial religions.

Suggestions for Additional Reading

The following books, which have been deliberately restricted to the most accessible works in English, will supply the essential background for anyone wishing to delve more deeply into the problems related to the advent of civilization.

On the subject of prehistory in general, Grahame Clark's *World Prehistory: An Outline* (2nd ed.; Cambridge, 1969) is lucid, scholarly and, for its short length, remarkably comprehensive. Robert J. Braidwood, *Prehistoric Men* (7th ed.; New York, 1967) is primarily addressed to the nonspecialist. Some of Braidwood's conclusions are controversial, but the reader is given fair warning. Another work that attempts to present the data of specialists to the lay reader is *Prehistoric Societies* (New York, 1965) by Grahame Clark and Stuart Piggott. A spirited and amusing description of prehistoric society is William White Howell's *Back of History: The Story of Our Own Origin* (Toronto, 1954). V. Gordon Childe, *What Happened in History* (Harmondsworth, 1954) has been influential in shaping opinions on the prehistoric stages of human development, and F. Clark Howell's *Early Man* (New York, 1965) is commendable for its drawings. Another good "first book" for the reader is Chester A. Starr, *Early Man* (New York, 1973).

More detailed accounts can be found in François Bordes, *The Old Stone Age* (New York, 1968), which also contains excellent illustrations; M.C. Koenigswald, *Meeting Prehistoric Man* (New York, 1957); M. C. Burkitt, *The Old Stone Age* (3rd ed.; New York, 1956); and William Howell, *Mankind in the Making* (rev. ed.; New York, 1967).

On the role played by archaeologists in advancing our knowledge of the advent of civilization, one of the best general surveys is Glyn Daniel, *A Hundred Years of Archaeology* (London, 1950). Daniel also provides valuable information on the growth of archaeology from the status of treasure-hunting to a science in his *Origin and Growth of Archaeology* (Harmondsworth, 1967). Dated but still valuable is Adolf A. Michaelis, *A Century of Archaeological Discoveries* (London, 1908), which deals with discoveries in classical lands up to the nineteenth century. For more popular accounts of the history of archaeology, W. H. Boulton, *The Romance of Archaeology* (London, n.d.) and C. W. Ceram, *Gods, Graves and Scholars* (London, 1952) can be read with profit.

Perhaps one of the best introductory accounts of what the work of the archaeologist is all about is Kurt W. Marek, *The March of Archaeology* (New York, 1958). Kathleen M. Kenyon's *Beginning of Archaeology* (London, 1953) is a brief handbook of archaeological practices, and Stuart Piggott, *Approach to Archaeology* (London, 1959) is an excellent introduction to the uses and limitations of the subject. V. Gordon Childe, *Piecing Together the Past* (London, 1956) reflects some of the problems in interpreting physical evidence. Considerably more comprehensive than any of the previously listed works is Sir Mortimer Wheeler's *Archaeology from the Earth* (Oxford, 1954). Also helpful are O. G. S. Crawford, *Man and his Past* (London, 1921); V. Gordon Childe, *A Short Introduction to Archaeology* (London, 1952); J. G. D. Clark, *Archaeology and Society* (3rd ed.; London, 1957); Sigfried De Laet, *Archaeology and its Problems* (London, 1957); and R. J. C. Atkinson, *Field Archaeology* (2nd ed.; London, 1954).

For those who desire an uncomplicated introduction to anthropology, Ashley Montagu's *Man: His First Million Years* (New York, 1957) may be helpful. Clyde Kluckhohn's *Mirror of Man: The Relationship of Anthropology to Modern Life* (New York, 1957) is the best and most readable introduction to what the anthropologist tries to do, and Alfred L. Kroeber, *Anthropology: Race, Language, Culture, Psychology, Prehistory* (New York, 1948) is the most outstanding textbook on general anthropology. A classic discussion of the meaning of culture is Ruth Benedict, *Patterns of Culture* (New York, 1946). Although dated, two of the best all round textbooks on cultural anthropology are R. H. Lowie, *An Introduction to Cultural Anthropology* (New York, 1940), and Melville Herskovits, *Man and his Works: The Science of Cultural Anthropology* (New York, 1948). For the history of anthropology and its influence on the study of civilization A. C. Haddon and A. H. Quiggin, *History of Anthropology* (London, 1934); T. K. Penniman, *A Hundred Years of Anthropology* (2nd ed.; London, 1952); R. H. Lowie, *The History of Ethnological Theory* (London, 1937); and Stanly Casson, *The Discovery of Man* (London, 1939) are all germane.

On the subject of evolution Theodosius Dobzhansky's *Evolution, Genetics and Man* (New York, 1955) is an authoritative work on the mechanisms of evolution, and Ralph Linton's *The Study of Man* (New York, 1936), although dated, is one of the best introductions to the evolution of man. Carlton S. Coon's *The Story of Man* (New York, 1954) is a good first book for the nonspecialist on man from his hominid origins to primitive culture and beyond. Among the works on Darwin that would be beneficial are Loren Eisely, *Darwin's Century* (London, 1959); William Irvine, *Apes, Angels and Victorians* (London, 1955); and J. W. Judd, *The Coming of Evolution* (Cambridge, 1910). For more specific emphasis on the impact of scientific discoveries upon religious beliefs, C. C. Gillispie's *Genesis and Geology* (New York, 1959) is readable and has an excellent bibliography.

One of the specific problems of the specialist dealing with prehistory is that of dating evidence. William F. Libby's *Radiocarbon Dating* (2nd ed.; Chicago, 1955) is helpful in explaining some of the techniques employed. Although it is quite technical, F. E. Zeuner's *Dating the Past* (4th ed.; London, 1958) would be profitable reading, and K. W. Butzer provides valuable information on the geological framework in his *Environment and Archaeology* (Chicago, 1964). David O. Woodbury, in *When the Ice Came* (New York, 1963), tries to explain the expansion of glaciers. Readers may also find it worthwhile to consult a more detailed account of the development and nature of our planet, such as John Verhoogen, *The Earth* (New York, 1970), or the more popular account, *The Earth We Live On* (New York, 1956), by Ruth Moore.

There are several excellent works that provide information on specific aspects of prehistoric life. The making of stone tools is explained by K. P. Oakley, *Man the Tool Maker* (2nd ed.; Chicago, 1957), and is told in a more amusing fashion by H. Mewhinney, *A Manual for Neanderthals* (Austin, 1957). The relationship between tool-making and the advent of civilization is discussed by V. Gordon Childe, *Man Makes Himself* (London, 1936); J. G. D. Clarke, *Prehistoric Europe: The Economic Basis* (London, 1952); I. W. Cornwall, *The World of Ancient Man* (New York, 1964); and *Prehistoric Animals and their Hunters* (London, 1968), also by Cornwall. Stuart Stuever, ed., *Prehistoric Agriculture* (New York, 1971); Don and Patricia Bothwell, *Food in Antiquity* (New York, 1969); and Sonia Cole, *The Neolithic Revolution* (3rd ed.; London, 1967) all reflect the agricultural advancement of prehistoric man and its consequence. An authoritative account by experts of the technological growth of man from the earliest times to the fall of the ancient empires can be found in Charles Singer et al., eds., *A History of Technology,* Vol. I (New York, 1954). Henry Hodges, *Technology in the Ancient World* (New York, 1970) is concise, and the development of metallurgy is explained in R. J. Forbes, *Metallurgy in Antiquity* (Leiden, 1950).

An extremely interesting and readable discussion of nonliterate man as a thinker is Paul Radin, *Primitive Man as Philosopher* (New York, 1927), and the controversial issue of race is covered in Richard Goldsby, *Race and Races* (New York, 1971). Additional information on the nature and quality of prehistoric life can be acquired from some of the very good anthologies and readers that have appeared over the last decade. Harry L. Shapiro, *Man, Culture and Society* (New York, 1960), and Sherwood L. Washburn, *Social Life of Early Man* (Chicago, 1961), both contain clear, descriptive essays and good bibliographies.

A survey of cave art can be found in Hans-Georg Bandi et al., *The Art of the Stone Age* (New York, 1961), and in *Paleolithic Cave Art* (New York, 1967), by Peter J. Ucko and Andrée Rosenfeld. Georges Bataille, *Lascaux* (New York, 1955) is a specialized study of one of the more famous cave-art sites.

On the emergence of civilization there are several excellent studies. Two very fine introductions are those of Henri Frankfort, *The Birth of Civilization in the Near East* (New York, 1956), and *Before Philosophy* (Harmondsworth, 1949). Jacquetta Hawkes and Sir Leonard Woolley, *Prehistory and the Beginning of Civilization* (London, 1963) contains excellent material dealing with primitive culture and the transition to higher civilization. Another work that is a good introduction to the history of the ancient world and is especially helpful for understanding prehistoric culture is Ralph E. Turner, *The Great Cultural Tradition: The Foundation of Civilization* (2 Vols.; New York, 1941). A thought-provoking work is Robert J. Braidwood, *The Near East and the Foundation for Civilization* (Eugene, 1952), and Stuart Piggott, ed., *The Dawn of Civilization* (London, 1961) is recommended for its illustrations. A good general survey of the Near East is William W. Hallo and William Kelly Simpson, *The Ancient Near East: A History* (New York, 1971).

Ancient civilization in Mesopotamia is well covered in Sabatino Moscati, *The Face of the Ancient Orient* (Chicago, 1960). His generous and pertinent selections from original source material provides flavor and weight to this valuable study. A. Leo Oppenheim's *Ancient Mesopotamia* (Chicago, 1964) is not an easy book to read but the general reader, with sufficient effort and patience, will find his effort rewarded. More readable and abundantly illustrated is M. E. L. Mallowan, *Early Mesopotamia and Iran* (London, 1965). Archaeological work in Mesopotamia is discussed in Seton Lloyd's *Foundations in the Dust* (London, 1947). An excellent summation of the contributions made by the Sumerians to history is Samuel Noah Kramer, *History Begins at Sumer* (London, 1958), and for more detailed information on the Sumerians by the same author see *The Sumerians: their History, Culture and Character* (Chicago, 1963).

More specialized treatment of Mesopotamia can be found in C. Leonard Woolley, *Ur of the Chaldees* (2nd ed.; Harmondsworth, 1950), which is a description of the excavation and findings of the ancient Sumerian city of Ur. Edward Chiera, *They Wrote on Clay* (Chicago, 1956) is a discussion, written for the nonspecialist, of the highly technical subject of ancient Babylonian writing. A brief but thorough description of religion of the peoples of the Tigris-Euphrates valley is available in S. H. Hooke, *Babylonian and Assyrian Religion* (Norman, 1963). H. W. F. Saggs, *The Greatness that Was Babylon* (London, 1962), and George Contenau, *Everyday Life in Babylonia and Assyria* (New York, 1965), are interesting and thorough examinations of the main features of Babylonian civilization treated topically.

The most illuminating work on Egyptian civilization is John A. Wilson, *Culture of Ancient Egypt* (Chicago, 1956). This work, previously published as *The Burden of Egypt* (1951), has no serious competitors as an evaluation of the Egyptian mentality and pattern of values. James A. Breasted, *A History of Egypt* (New York, 1912) is now out of date in specific details, but is still useful for its penetrating insights and profound understanding. An excellent supplement to Breasted is G. Steindorff and Kenneth Seele, *When Egypt Ruled the East* (2nd ed.; Chicago, 1956), which is rich in quotations from ancient Egyptian documents. Cyril Aldred, *The Egyptians* (New York, 1963) is a briefer account. The most satisfactory study of Egypt before the rule of the dynasties is Elsie Baumgartel, *The Culture of Prehistoric Egypt* (London, 1955). Barbara Mertz's *Red Land, Black Land* (New York, 1966) treats Egyptian life and death, while Henri Frankfort's *Ancient Egyptian Religion* (New York, 1961) is a sophisticated treatment of Egyptian religion. Expert essays on subjects germane to this study can be found in R. K. Glanville, ed., *The Legacy of Egypt* (London, 1942). Herman Kees, in *Ancient Egypt* (Chicago, 1961), describes in detail particular Egyptian cities, and daily life in Egypt is covered by Pierre Montel, *Everyday Life in Egypt* (Harmondsworth, 1958).